William C. Roberts

The Leading Orators of Twenty-Five Campaigns from the First Presidential Canvass to the Present Time

Vol. 1

William C. Roberts

The Leading Orators of Twenty-Five Campaigns from the First Presidential Canvass to the Present Time
Vol. 1

ISBN/EAN: 9783337813826

Printed in Europe, USA, Canada, Australia, Japan

Cover: Foto ©ninafisch / pixelio.de

More available books at **www.hansebooks.com**

THE

LEADING ORATORS

OF TWENTY-FIVE CAMPAIGNS,

From the First Presidential Canvass

TO THE PRESENT TIME.

PORTRAITS, REMINISCENCES, AND
BIOGRAPHICAL SKETCHES OF

AMERICA'S DISTINGUISHED POLITICAL SPEAKERS.

A CONCISE HISTORY OF
POLITICAL PARTIES IN THE UNITED STATES, TOGETHER WITH
A CHRONOLOGICAL PRESENTATION OF PRESIDENTIAL
AND VICE-PRESIDENTIAL NOMINEES.

BY

WILLIAM C. ROBERTS.

———•———

NEW YORK:
L. K. STROUSE & CO., PUBLISHERS,
95 NASSAU STREET.
1884.

INDEX.

POLITICAL PARTIES	7
ADAMS, JOHN	42
ADAMS, SAMUEL	26
BEECHER, HENRY WARD	128
BLAINE, JAMES G	243
BURLINGAME, ANSON	149
BURR, AARON	33
BUTLER, BENJAMIN F	205
CALHOUN, JOHN C	64
CARD, ALBERT MILLER	218
CASS, LEWIS	109
CHOATE, RUFUS	84
CLAY, HENRY	52
COLFAX, SCHUYLER	130
CONKLING, ROSCOE	197
CORWIN, THOMAS	102
CURTIS, GEORGE WILLIAM	160
CUSHING, CALEB	94
DAVIS, HENRY WINTER	120
DEPEW, CHAUNCEY M	246
DICKENSON, DANIEL S	110
DOUGHERTY, DANIEL	170
DOUGLASS, FREDERICK	134
DOUGLAS, STEPHEN A	146
EVARTS, WILLIAM M	179
EVERETT, EDWARD	81
EWING, THOMAS	72
FESSENDEN, WILLIAM PITT	105
GARFIELD, JAMES A	226
GROW, GALUSHA A	168
HAMILTON, ALEXANDER	37
HAMPTON, WADE	204
HANCOCK, JOHN	21
HARRISON, CARTER H	196
HENDRICKS, THOMAS A	214
HENRY, PATRICK	20
HUBBARD, RICHARD B	184
INGERSOLL, ROBERT G	248
KILPATRICK, HUGH JUDSON	194
LEE, RICHARD HENRY	27
LINCOLN, ABRAHAM	144
LOGAN, JOHN A	220
MAHONE, WILLIAM	237
MARSHALL, THOMAS	116
PHILLIPS, WENDELL	90
PRENTISS, SARGEANT S	96
RANDOLPH, JOHN	48
SCHURZ, CARL	216
SEYMOUR, HORATIO	166
SEWARD, WILLIAM H	153
SCHENCK, ROBERT C	137
SHERMAN, JOHN	234
SUMNER, CHARLES	123
VAN BUREN, MARTIN	57
WEBSTER, DANIEL	68
WILLIAMS, GEORGE H	183
WIRT, WILLIAM	78
WOODFORD, STEWART L	207
YOUMANS, LEROY F	229

LIST OF PORTRAITS.

		PAGE
1.	THOMAS CORWIN	*Frontispiece*
2.	DANIEL S. DICKENSON	17
3.	WENDELL PHILLIPS	31
4.	HENRY WARD BEECHER	45
5.	FREDERICK DOUGLASS	59
6.	GEORGE WILLIAM CURTIS	73
7.	HORATIO SEYMOUR	87
8.	DANIEL DOUGHERTY	99
9.	WILLIAM M. EVARTS	111
10.	RICHARD B. HUBBARD	121
11.	HUGH JUDSON KILPATRICK	131
12.	ROSCOE CONKLING	141
13.	WADE HAMPTON	151
14.	BENJAMIN F. BUTLER	161
15.	STEWART L. WOODFORD	171
16.	CARL SCHURZ	181
17.	ALBERT MILLER CARD	191
18.	LEROY F. YOUMANS	201
19.	WILLIAM MAHONE	211
20.	JAMES G. BLAINE	221
21.	CHAUNCEY M. DEPEW	231
22.	ROBERT G. INGERSOLL	241

POLITICAL PARTIES IN THE UNITED STATES.

PARTY issues were not clearly drawn until the beginning of the Revolutionary War, when the question arose on what terms the colonies should continue their relations with England.

WHIG PARTY.

Whig and Tory then became the respective party designations, after factions which bore those appellations in England.

The former wished to remain colonists with guaranteed rights, while the latter were willing to continue that relation under such dispensation as the Crown saw fit to extend.

The Whigs, early in 1776, took advanced ground, and advocated absolute separation from Great Britain, while the Tories held to royal allegiance.

Step by step this progressive party moved toward the dawning liberty which it saw beyond the clouds of British subjection, and on the 7th of June it moved, in Congress, the resolution of separation, and on the 4th of July following the Declaration of Independence was adopted.

The Whigs fought for a cause as righteous as any which ever arrayed men in combat, and after years of struggle they won a victory which the prophetic patriots could not then compass, and which, more than a century later, is without a boundary line. The Whig party fulfilled the mission for which it was organized, and in 1787 ceased to exist.

TORY PARTY.

The Tory party was composed of the timid and conservative who feared the strength of England, and who had misgivings of the ultimate success of the patriots—a large professional class dependent upon royal landholders and all the royal officers.

The party died with the Revolution in 1783, when its members, such as had not been put to death, banished, exiled or transported, or had not abandoned the United States, commingled with the Whigs.

When the issues of the Revolution were substantially settled, the Whig party, the only one from 1783 to 1787, became divided as to the best means of establishing a national government.

One faction, called Particularists, held that State government should be supreme, while the other, styled *Strong* Government men, maintained that local self-government was inadequate to meet the public service, which could only be controlled through a central power.

From a discussion of these questions, as to the best basis for a government of the United States, developed the Federal and anti-Federal parties in 1787.

FEDERAL PARTY.

The Federal party advocated a Constitution and the anti-Federal party a Confederation.

The condition of the country at this period, with threatened anarchy and civil war, gave strength to the measure advocated by the Federalists, and by the adoption of the Constitution in 1778 they won their first party victory.

They developed into Broad Constructionists, desiring to interpret the Constitution in such a manner as would invest the Federal Government with the greatest amount of power.

The Federal party was in the minority until the election of Washington to the Presidency, when the prestige of his name gave it numerical strength, and the reins of government passed into its hands.

As a party, the Federalists maintained an existence for nearly thirty-three years, during which time it settled the form of government under the Constitution, elected and controlled the administration of Washington during two terms, and of Adams during one term.

The election, in 1800, of Jefferson, the Republican nominee, broke the sceptre of Federal power, and in name only it maintained an existence for twenty years thereafter, when its members commingled with the Republicans.

ANTI-FEDERAL PARTY.

The anti-Federalists, formerly known as Particularists, were the dominant faction until the adoption of the Constitution. This name they were given by their opponents, because they opposed a Federal government under the Constitution. When that measure was adopted the anti-Federalists became close Constructionists, desiring to interpret the Constitution in its most literal sense.

DEMOCRATIC REPUBLICAN PARTY.

In 1789-90 the Constitution had gained such popularity that the minority withdrew all opposition, and vied with its founders in promoting its beneficent objects. They claimed to be the true friends of Republican government and the advocates of popular institutions, and rejected, as inappropriate, the anti-Federal name, and assumed the title of Democratic Republican.

In 1791 the name "Democratic" was generally dropped, and the organization, a direct outgrowth from the anti-Federal party, was known as the Republican party. (For party nominations and elections in 1796, see Chapter III.)

The Republican or Democratic-Republican party was in existence from 1791 until 1828.

It elevated Thomas Jefferson to the Vice-Presidency in 1796; promoted him to the Presidency in 1800; re-elected him in 1804; chose Madison as his successor in 1808; elected Madison in 1812; elected and supported Monroe two terms, and selected John Quincy Adams as his successor in 1824.

From 1817 to 1828 this organization was substantially the only party in existence, it having absorbed the last of the Federalists at the close of the campaign in 1820.

CLINTONIAN PARTY.

In 1812 a faction broke out of the Republican party which opposed the monopoly which Virginia had acquired in supplying executive officers, and to the caucus system, which disfranchised the people from selecting candidates, and who were also dissatisfied with the foreign policy of the Administration.

This movement was led by De Witt Clinton, and his supporters were called "Clintonians."

This element returned to the Republican fold in 1815. (See Chapter XII.)

PEACE PARTY.

The Peace party came from the ranks of the Federalists in 1812. Their ostensible aim was for the purpose of instilling in the minds of the people the benign doctrines of peace, but their professions were mistrusted, and it was believed their ulterior purpose was to oppose the war and array the religious sentiment of the country against the Administration.

The Washington Benevolent Society was established at about the same time, having similar objects in view.

ANTI-MASONIC PARTY.

In September, 1826, William Morgan, a royal arch- Mason, threatened to publish the "secrets" of Masonry. He was arrested for a debt of two dollars, and placed in jail, from which he was taken at night by men whose identity has never been discovered, and conveyed to Fort Niagara. He disappeared on the 29th of the same month, and was never seen afterward.

Great excitement followed this occurrence, as it was charged the Masons had put him to death. The following year the subject was launched into politics, and the anti-Masonic party was organized, which found a few supporters in all the principal towns and cities of the country. The object of the party was the suppression of secret societies and the exclusion from office of their supporters. It held an existence from 1827 until 1834, when it became a constituent with the Nullification and National Republican organizations, which formed the Whig party in that year. (See Chapter XII.)

DEMOCRATIC PARTY.

A division occurred in the Republican party in 1827, and the faction which supported General Jackson dropped the name of Republican and adopted the title "Democratic" "as a novel, distinct, and popular name, in 1828." This marks the date of the birth of the present Democratic party, though until 1836 its adherents were generally called "Jackson men." The members of this new organization, being close Constructionists, claimed political lineage from Jefferson.

POLITICAL PARTIES IN THE UNITED STATES.

The Democrats elected General Jackson, their first candidate, in 1828, and re-elected him in 1832. They gained another victory with Van Buren in 1836, and met with defeat against General Harrison, the Whig nominee, in 1840. With James K. Polk they were again victorious in 1844, and suffered defeat with their candidate, Lewis Cass, in 1848. Franklin Pierce led the party again to power in 1852, and their candidate, James Buchanan, was inaugurated in 1857. They lost control of the Government in 1861, and in six successive elections they have failed to seat a President.

It will therefore be seen that this great party has held a dominant influence over the politics of the nation for more than half a century.

NATIONAL REPUBLICAN PARTY.

The faction of the Republican party which adhered to Adams in 1827, when the division in that party occurred, retained the name Republican, to which they prefixed the "National" in 1828, to indicate the national character of their principles in contradistinction from the sectional policy which it was charged the Jackson or Democratic party upheld.

This party presented Presidential candidates in 1828 and 1832, and suffered defeat at both elections. It merged into the Whig party in 1834, when its name became extinct. (See Chapters XI. and XII.)

NULLIFICATION PARTY.

In 1831, after the disruption which occurred in President Jackson's cabinet, John C. Calhoun set out to organize a party of his own. He visited the States of Georgia and South Carolina, and sought to array the slave power against the Administration, and advised resistance to tariff enactments. Nullification was the principal doctrine which he advocated, and his party bore that name.

He drew but a meagre following, and in 1833 his organization disbanded, when part of his followers returned to the Democratic party, and the balance found refuge with the Whigs in 1834.

WHIG PARTY.

In 1834 three parties—the National Republican, anti-Mason, and Nullification—converged and formed the Whig party. This movement was induced by intense political excitement, occasioned by President Jackson's order to remove the "deposits," and many Democrats joined the Whig ranks.

In 1836 the Whigs nominated General Harrison, who met with defeat. He was presented to the people again in 1840, and was elected. Four years later Henry Clay was given the nomination, and was retired without Presidential honors.

General Taylor was nominated in 1848, and carried the election.

General Scott was the last candidate of this party, and was defeated by Franklin Pierce in the election of 1852. After this election the party became disorganized and shortly disbanded, its members finding shelter in various camps which at that time were located on the political field.

LOCOFOCO PARTY.

In 1835 a fragment of the Democratic party, which styled themselves the "Equal-Rights" party, held a meeting in Tammany Hall, New York. In the midst of great confusion which prevailed, the lights were extinguished. The room was immediately relighted with candles and locofoco matches. From this circumstance the name of Locofoco was for a time applied to the Democratic party by the opposition.

ABOLITION PARTY.

Various causes conduced to the organization of this party in 1839. The sympathy felt for slaves, and the measures taken in Congress to suppress petitions in their behalf, were leading elements in its formation. The anti-Slavery Society, organized in 1833, and which dissolved in 1839, composed the major portion of the membership of the Abolition party.

This party held a convention at Warsaw, N. Y., in the fall of 1839 (see Chapter XIV.), and in 1840 dropped its distinctive name for Liberty party.

LIBERTY PARTY.

In 1840 the Abolition party underwent a change of name, and Liberty party was the title adopted. Its principles continued the same. It had immediate accessions from both the Whig and Democratic ranks. It held national conventions in 1843 and 1847 (see Chapters XV. and XVI.), and merged into the Free Soil party in 1848.

POLITICAL PARTIES IN THE UNITED STATES. 13

BARNBURNERS AND HUNKERS.

These titles were bestowed upon two factions of the Democratic party in the State of New York.

Disagreement in the Legislature, in 1843, over some minor questions invited a party rupture, which led to irreconcilable estrangement between the factions, and in the Polk canvass of 1844 they were given the respective names of Barnburners and Hunkers.

NATIVE AMERICAN PARTY.

In 1843 some illiberal-minded men, becoming alarmed at the great inflow of foreigners to some of the principal American ports, organized to disfranchise Catholics and immigrants from holding public offices. Its followers were generally styled "Natives." It passed out of existence in 1852.

THE FREE-SOIL PARTY

was made up of the Liberal party and the Barnburners, who retired from the Democratic Convention held in Baltimore in 1848. It held two national conventions, developed little strength, and expired about the year 1855.

SILVER-GRAY PARTY.

At a Whig State Convention held at Syracuse in September, 1850, a resolution was introduced which declared that William H. Seward deserved the thanks of the convention for the fidelity with which he had sustained, in the United States Senate, the liberal and long-cherished principles of the Whig party. At this William Duer, a member of Congress and a supporter of the Administration, proclaimed that if the resolution were adopted the Whig party would be broken up. The resolution was adopted, and the delegates who opposed such an indorsement of Mr. Seward's course, together with the chairman, withdrew from the convention, and assembled in another hall, and called a convention of President Fillmore's friends to meet at Utica on the 17th of October following. The delegates met agreeably to call, renounced allegiance to the Whigs, and organized a party which they christened the "Silver Gray." The party approved the President's course. Its life, like that of all parties which had sprung from personal and factional animosity, was short.

AMERICAN PARTY.

Substantially the same motives which induced the organization of the Native American party in 1843 contributed to the formation of the American party in 1852. In fact, it may be said it was the same organization, proclaiming the same doctrines under a new name. Added to the old creed was the "purification of the ballot-box" and the retention of the Bible in the public schools. Its members were sworn to support the candidates nominated by the order. It was generally called the Know-Nothing party, because, when interrogated concerning their order, the members replied they knew nothing.

KNOW-NOTHING PARTY.

(*See American Party.*)

REPUBLICAN PARTY.

In 1854, when the repeal of the Missouri Compromise was proposed, the people were aroused to a profound degree that an assault upon liberty was attempted.

This awakened earnest discussion from the pulpit, the platform, and the press, and large numbers of anti-Slavery men belonging to the different parties held the conviction that success could be secured only "through the formation of a new party, which could act without the embarrassment of a pro-slavery wing." The first steps toward the organization of such a party was during the early months of 1854, at Ripon, Fond du Lac County, Wisconsin. A meeting was then held on the last of February, which adopted a resolution that if the Kansas-Nebraska Bill should pass they would "throw old party organizations aside and organize a new party on the sole issue of the non-extension of slavery." A meeting was held at the same place on the 20th of March following, and the sentiment was in favor of adopting the name of "Republican." The movement thus initiated perfected a party organization in that State at a convention held the following July. A leading journal in Detroit "took ground in favor of disbanding the Whig and Free-Soil parties, and of the organization of a

POLITICAL PARTIES IN THE UNITED STATES. 15

new party composed of all the opponents of slavery extension." The resound of this declaration was a mass convention held in Michigan on the 6th of July, which adopted a platform opposing the extension of slavery.

About the year 1853, by a fusion of Whigs, Free Soilers, anti-Nebraska Democrats, and anti-Slavery Americans, the organization of the Republican party was perfected.

General Fremont, the party's first Presidential nominee, met with defeat in 1856.

Lincoln carried the election in 1860, and since his inauguration, in 1861, the party has been in power.

LABOR-REFORM PARTY.

Societies, which were called "Trades Union," organized in most of the cities throughout the country, had for their objects reforms looking to a greater equality of condition among the people.

In 1872 they had gained such proportions as to make themselves felt in national politics, and in that sphere they acquired the title of the Labor-Reform party. (See Chapter XXII.)

Later on an element with communistic tendencies ingratiated themselves, to a certain extent, in the favor of this party, with questionable advantage for its good.

LIBERAL REPUBLICAN PARTY.

This organization grew from a faction which left the Republican party, in 1870, dissatisfied with the Grant administration and the course of the party at that time.

It developed into national importance in 1871, and presented a Presidential ticket in 1872. (See Chapter XXII.)

TEMPERANCE PARTY.

Temperance societies, which have been in existence all over the country for many years, combined their forces in 1872, and assumed a national party existence. In 1876 the name was changed to Prohibition Reform party.

THE NATIONAL GREENBACK PARTY.

The "hard times" which followed the financial disturbances of 1873 gave birth to the inflation theories advocated by this party.

They urged an increase of the paper money of the Government, claiming such action would prevent immense losses by the depreciation of values. They also contended that the paper money issued by the Government should never be redeemed, but should be "coined paper," made, by the authority of the Government, good for all debts, public and private.

The party made Presidential nominations in 1876 and 1880. (See Chapters XXIII. and XXIV.)

DANIEL S. DICKENSON.

CHAPTER I.

CAMPAIGN OF 1788.

FEDERAL NOMINEES.

For President.
GEORGE WASHINGTON of Virginia.

For Vice-President.
JOHN ADAMS of Massachusetts.
JOHN JAY of New York.
JOHN RUTLEDGE of South Carolina.

ANTI-FEDERAL NOMINEES.

For Vice-President.
JOHN HANCOCK of Massachusetts.
SAMUEL ADAMS of Massachusetts.
GEORGE CLINTON of New York.

THE Continental Congress, in September, 1788, set the first Wednesday of January, 1789, for the choice of Presidential electors, the first Wednesday of February for the electoral choice of a President and Vice-President of the United States, and the first Wednesday (4th day) of March for inaugurating the new Government.

Fortunately for the Union at that critical period, there was one man in America to whom all eyes instinctively turned, and upon whom the country leaned for guidance in this new experience with equal confidence and safety.

George Washington, by the voice of the eleven States which had then ratified the Constitution, was the chosen candidate for the Presidency, without a competitor.

It was for the Vice-Presidency that the ambitious men of that time thirsted, an office clearly of empty honor in itself, but thought to carry a valuable estate in expectancy. Pennsylvania presented no candidates for the office, and New York had forfeited all claims upon it by reason of her Legislature failing to agree on the mode of choosing electors. Eleven candidates received electoral votes for the office of Vice-President.

PATRICK HENRY.

Patrick Henry, one of America's most distinguished natural orators, was born at Studley, Hanover County, Virginia, May 29th, 1736.

With a very limited and imperfect education, he commenced life as an agriculturist, and failing to earn a livelihood in that vocation, by the assistance of his father and father-in-law he was started in a store.

It was soon discovered that the future orator possessed none of the traits which secure success in trade.

He was indolent and careless, and in two or three years the store was closed, and Patrick Henry, the merchant, was insolvent. After this experience he vacillated between cultivating the soil and keeping store, alternately failing in both occupations, until the age of twenty-four, when he began the study of law.

After six weeks' study he presented himself before the judges, who granted him a license with hesitation, and only after a promise to study further before commencing practice. He had no clients, and it is related that the distress of his family became extreme.

At the age of twenty-seven he was retained in a case which seemed so hopeless that it was not deemed worth while to employ a better advocate. The controversy, in which the clergy were a party, was touching the emoluments to which they were entitled under the law of the Established Church of England in Virginia. Their case was lucidly and calmly stated by Peter Lyons, a distinguished counsellor of the time, and Patrick Henry rose to reply. The array before him was terrifying, and the presence of his father in the chair of presiding magistrate increased his embarrassment. His exordium was awkward and confused. He visibly faltered. The crowd, whose sympathies were all on the side which he represented, hung their heads and gave up the contest. The clergy smiled and exchanged glances of triumph. The father of the speaker bowed his head in mortification. But suddenly the spell was changed. Patrick Henry, by some mysterious and almost supernatural transformation, stood anew in the presence of his auditors, the foremost orator in the land.

Those who heard him in this speech said that he " made their blood to run cold and their hair to stand on end." Under his terrible invective the clergy were driven from the room, and the jury, after retiring for an instant, brought in a verdict of only one penny damages. Thus, at a single step, Patrick Henry rose to the first rank among the orators of the time.

Momentous events followed in rapid succession his rise to eminence, and at the age of twenty-nine he had gained the reputation of being the greatest orator and political thinker of a land abounding with public speakers and statesmen.

In 1788 he was a member of the convention to ratify the Federal Constitution, but he opposed it with all the strength and eloquence of his youth. Although his opposition afterward abated in a measure, he always remained fearful that the final result would be the destruction of the rights of States.

In politics he was a Whig, an anti-Federalist, and a Republican. Patrick Henry was undoubtedly one of the most extraordinary men of an extraordinary epoch. In the House of Burgesses he was without a peer. In the General Congress the men of the North acknowledged that Patrick Henry was the greatest orator whom they had ever heard. To that mysterious eloquence which swayed and took captive all minds he united a nerve and resolution which were indomitable. As a mere logician, apart from the advocate, Henry had no conspicuous talent. He lives and will always live as the orator of the Revolution, who voiced most boldly and clearly the principles of human freedom.

JOHN HANCOCK.

The Declaration of Independence, though signed by all the members of the Congress, was accompanied, in its first publication, by the signature of John Hancock alone—an accidental association, which, although it conferred no special title to praise beyond his colleagues, preoccupied the admiration of the public, and has contributed, in no small degree, to the extension of his fame. The boldness of the writing rendered it conspicuous, and to this day it is synonymous with a brave and fearless writer, who has nothing to conceal, and takes all risk.

John Hancock, son of a gentleman of the same name, was born January 12th, 1737, near the present village of Quincy, Massachusetts. This same village gave birth to Samuel Adams ; and besides furnishing two of our chief magistrates, may be noted for the production of three of the most distinguished characters of the Revolution.

Under the care of his uncle John Hancock received his education, graduating from Harvard College in 1754, and immediately entered as a clerk in the counting-house of his uncle. In 1760 he visited England, was present at the funeral of George II. and at the coronation of his successor. Soon after his return to America, at the age of twenty-seven years, by inheritance from his uncle, he became possessed of a vast property.

He was first chosen selectman of the town of Boston, an office which he held many years, and was elected in 1766, with James Otis, Samuel Adams, and Thomas Cushing, a representative to the General Assembly of the province. In 1766 his sloop Liberty was seized for contravention of the commercial laws, and in the riot which followed the royal customs commissioners barely escaped with their lives. After the massacre of Boston, in 1770, he inveighed with much spirit against the troops, demanding their removal from the town, and five years afterward the attempt to seize his person led to the first revolutionary battle at Concord, Massachusetts. In 1774 Hancock was President of the Provincial Congress at Philadelphia. Returning to Massachusetts, he assisted in framing the Constitution, and in 1780 was chosen first governor. He was annually elected to this dignity till 1785, and again from 1787 to 1793, sitting as an ordinary member of the Legislature in the interval. He died suddenly at Quincy, October 8th, 1793.

Such is the condensed record of an active life during times of intense excitement.

During the first provocations of the British Government, by which she excited discontent and opposition in her colonies, his diligence and talents were exerted conspicuously. It was by his agency and that of a few other citizens of Boston that, for the purpose of causing such duties to be revoked, associations were instituted to prohibit the importation of British goods—a policy which, soon afterward, being imitated in the other colonies, first kindled the apprehensions and awoke the vigilance of the people to the preservation of their liberties. In 1769 the Governor of the province introduced into Boston several regiments of British troops, a measure that, more than all others, served to irritate the inhabitants and nourish the seeds of rebellion.

On the evening of the 5th of March, 1770, a small party of British soldiers parading in King Street, Boston, were assailed with balls of snow and other accidental weapons by a tumultuary assemblage of citizens, who, by order of the commanding officer, were repelled with a discharge of musketry, and several of the crowd were wounded and a few were killed. This affray, which is usually termed "the massacre of Boston," although originating in the provocations of the people, was regarded as an act of atrocious iniquity, which required an immediate and signal revenge. An assembly of the citizens was convened on the succeeding day, in which Mr. Hancock, with some others, was appointed to request of the governor a removal of the British troops from the town.

The bodies of the slain being, a few days after their decease, borne to the place of burial, were deposited in the same tomb. The speech delivered by Mr. Hancock upon this occasion was a bold and burning denunciation of tyranny. The following extract may be given as a specimen of its style and temper:

"But I gladly quit this theme of death—I would not dwell too long upon the horrid effects which have already followed from quartering regular troops in this town. Standing armies are sometimes composed of persons unfit to live in civil society; who are equally indifferent to the glory of a George or a Louis; who, for the addition of one penny a day to their wages, would desert from the Christian cross and fight under the crescent of the Turkish Sultan; from such men as these, what has not a State to fear? With such as these usurping Cæsar passed the Rubicon; with such as these he humbled mighty Rome, and forced the mistress of the world to own a master in a traitor. These are the men whom sceptred robbers now employ to frustrate the designs of God, and render vain the bounties which His gracious hand pours upon His creatures."

In 1775 it was proposed by the American officers to bombard the city of Boston. This would have financially ruined Mr. Hancock, but with magnificent patriotism he said that "his private fortune should, on no occasion, be an obstacle to the interests of his country."

In stature Mr. Hancock was above the middle size. Of excellent proportion of limbs, a benign countenance ; possessing a flexible and harmonious voice, a manly and dignified aspect.

As an orator Mr. Hancock spoke without elaboration or pretension, but agreeably on all subjects. His harangues exhibit no common comprehension of things or powers of language, and were especially well suited to the dispositions of the times in which he lived. In his private and social life he was passionately addicted to what were then called the "elegant pleasures"—dancing, music, concerts, routs, assemblies, card parties, rich wines, social dinners, and festivities. His equipage was magnificent, and such as at present is unknown in America. His apparel was sumptuously embroidered with gold, silver, and lace ; he rode with six beautiful bays and with servants in livery. It is no trivial commendation that, possessing a superfluity of wealth, he betook himself to honorable and laborious pursuits, and that arrogance or insolence were foreign to his kindly nature.

PRESIDENT WASHINGTON'S FIRST CABINET.

Secretary of State.—Thomas Jefferson, of Virginia, appointed September 26th, 1789.

Secretary of the Treasury.—Alexander Hamilton, of New York, appointed September 11th, 1789.

Secretary of War and of the Navy.—Henry Knox, of Massachusetts, appointed September 12th, 1789.

Attorney-General.—Edmund Randolph, of Virginia, appointed September 26th, 1789.

CHAPTER II.

CAMPAIGN OF 1792.

FEDERAL NOMINEES.

For President.

GEORGE WASHINGTON of Virginia.

For Vice-President.

JOHN ADAMS of Massachusetts.

REPUBLICAN NOMINEES.

For Vice-President.

GEORGE CLINTON of New York.
THOMAS JEFFERSON of Virginia.
AARON BURR of New York.

CAUCUSES AND NOMINATIONS.

CAUCUSES were held in 1792 by both parties at the seat of Government, then located at Philadelphia. Washington's administration had been so acceptable that he was nominated for a second term without opposition in his own party, and the Republicans made no nomination for that office. John Adams was placed in nomination by the Federalists for a second Vice-Presidential term, and three candidates were named by the Republicans for that position.

The election gave General Washington the entire electoral vote for the Presidency, while John Adams only received eleven votes more than a majority.

SAMUEL ADAMS.

Since the formation of our Government, in some one of the public walks of life, the Adams have made their presence felt. While a few members of this distinguished family have succeeded in work alien from that generally denominated "political," their bent and hereditary talent has drawn them easily and naturally into politics, and with wealth, education, and honorable ambition their successes will not seem strange to the careful student.

Samuel Adams was born at Boston, Massachusetts, September 27th, 1722, thus being a native of the same commonwealth as John Adams, his second cousin.

He studied at Harvard, but owing to his father's misfortunes in business, in connection with a banking speculation—the "manufactory scheme"—he had to leave before completing his course, and to relinquish his intention of becoming a Congregational clergyman. He received his degree as A. M., however, and it is worthy of note, as showing the tendency of his political opinions at that time—1743—that his thesis was a defence of the affirmative reply to the question, "Whether it be lawful to resist the supreme magistrate, if the commonwealth cannot otherwise be preserved?"

The failure of the banking scheme above referred to, in consequence of the limitations imposed by English law, made Adams still more decided in his assertion of the rights of American citizens, and in his opposition to Parliament.

He gave up his business, in which he had little success, and became tax-collector for the city of Boston, whence he was called by his political opponents "Samuel the publican."

In all the proceedings which found issuance at last in the Declaration of Independence, Mr. Adams was a conspicuous actor. He took part in the numerous town meetings, drafted the protest which was sent up by Boston against the taxation scheme of Grenville (May, 1764), and being chosen next year a member of the General Court of Massachusetts, soon became one of the leaders in debate. Upon his entry into the house he was appointed clerk, and had much influence in arranging the order of business and framing enactments. Attempts were more than once made by the English Governor to win him over by the offer of a place, but he proved inflexible.

His uncompromising resistance to the British Government continued; he was a prominent member of the Continental Congress at Philadelphia, and was one of those who signed the Declaration of Independence in 1776. He took an active part in framing the Constitution of the State of Massachusetts, and was for several years President of the Senate of that State. He held the office of its lieutenant-governor from 1789 to 1794, and governor from 1794 to 1797, retiring from public life the latter year, partly on account of age, but partly also because the Federalists were then in the ascendant, and he himself was inclined to the Jefferson, or Republican party. He died at Boston October 3d, 1803.

Some witty writer has said: "To steal my purse is wicked, but to appropriate my ideas is flattery. It shows appreciation." In an oration on American Independence, delivered in Philadelphia August 1st, 1776, Adams characterizes the English as "a nation of shopkeepers." The oration was translated into French, and published at Paris. It is not unlikely that Napoleon's use of this phrase was unintentional "flattery" of Mr. Adams.

Mr. Adams had great courage and determination, but at the same time was somewhat narrow-minded and bigoted, both in religion and politics. He was prejudiced against Washington, whose conduct of the war his ignorance of military matters led him to think weak and dilatory; and the confidence reposed in Washington, as first President of the Republic, seemed to him to savor of aristocracy. His personal honor was never doubted, even by the political enemies necessarily made in a long and active life.

RICHARD HENRY LEE.

The part borne by the Lee family, of Virginia, in the formation of our Republic, is second to none. Their ancestor, Richard Lee, emigrated, with a numerous household, to America, in the reign of King Charles I., and settled in the country lying between the Rappahannock and Potomac rivers. He was a bold Royalist, and during the Protectorate of Cromwell was mainly instrumental in inducing the colony of Virginia to assume a semi-independent attitude.

Among the descendants of this cavalier, all of whom were noted as scholars or statesmen, the most illustrious was Richard Henry Lee, his great-grandson, and one of the six distinguished sons of Thomas Lee.

Richard Henry Lee was born at Stratford, in Virginia, January 20th, 1732. After obtaining the foundation of a liberal education, first at home and afterward in England, he spent a little time in travel. Returning to Virginia in 1752, he came into the possession of a fine property left him by his father, and for several years thereafter applied himself to varied studies.

At the age of twenty-five he was appointed justice of the peace, and soon after was chosen a delegate to the House of Burgesses. He kept a diffident silence during two sessions, his first speech being in strong opposition to slavery, which he proposed to discourage, and eventually to abolish, by imposing a heavy tax on all further importations.

In 1764 Lee had applied for a collectorship under the Stamp Act, which afterward aroused the determined hostility of the colonies; but on reflection he regretted doing so, and became an outspoken promoter of the most extreme democratic ideas. He did not come prominently before his countrymen until after this act was passed; also the act of the British Parliament, in 1764, declaring its right to tax the colonies, when, associated with Patrick Henry, he immediately became the centre of an active opposition among the colonists of Virginia. In February, 1766, he organized an association in Westmoreland, in accordance with Patrick Henry's famous resolution against the Stamp Act, and at the winter session of the Burgesses, Lee, with the aid of Patrick Henry, succeeded in carrying the House upon a test question against the united aristocratic elements of the colony. In 1767 he spoke eloquently against the acts levying duties upon tea and other articles, and in 1768, in a letter to John Dickenson, of Pennsylvania, he made the suggestion of a private correspondence among the friends of liberty in the different colonies. Lee is said also to have originated, in conversation with fellow-patriots in 1773, the plan of an intercolonial or Continental Congress. He was soon after sent as a delegate from Virginia to the first American Congress, which met at Philadelphia September 5th, 1774, and at once became a leader in the assembly. He had the chief part in the composition of some of those addresses to the king, the people of England, and the colonies, which compelled the great Chatham to admit that, " for solidity of reasoning, force of sagacity, and wisdom of conclusion, under such complication of circumstances, no nation or body of men can stand in preference to the General Congress at Philadelphia."

Lee is known to have penned the second address to the people of Great Britain, which was among the most effective papers of the time.

When war between the colonies and the mother-country became inevitable, Lee was placed on the committees charged with preparing the munitions of war, and with devising all other means of offering a vigorous resistance to the British Government. His labors at this time were enormous.

On the 7th of June, 1776, Lee made the most celebrated and important of all his speeches, when introducing in Congress the resolution declaring "that these united colonies are, and of right ought to be, free and independent States, that they are absolved from all allegiance to the British crown, and that all political connection between them and the state of Great Britain is, and ought to be, totally dissolved."

During the War of Independence he was—in spite of ill-health—one of the most active of the patriotic party, chiefly, however, as a civilian. He was a member of the Congresses of 1778-80 and 1784-85. In 1784 he was elected President of Congress, and was one of the first Senators chosen from Virginia after the adoption of the Federal Constitution. Though strongly opposed to the adoption of that Constitution, owing to what he regarded as its dangerous infringements upon the independent power of the States, he accepted the place of Senator in hopes of bringing about amendments. He became a warm upholder of Washington's administration, and his prejudices against the Constitution were largely removed by its working in practice.

He retired from public life in 1792, and died in his native State, at Chantilly, Westmoreland County, June 19th, 1794.

PRESIDENT WASHINGTON'S SECOND CABINET.

Secretaries of State.—Thomas Jefferson, of Virginia, continued; Edmund Randolph, of Virginia, appointed January 2d, 1794; Timothy Pickering, of Massachusetts, appointed December 10th, 1795.

Secretaries of the Treasury.—Alexander Hamilton, of New York, continued; Oliver Wolcott, of Connecticut, appointed February 2d, 1795.

Secretaries of War and of the Navy.—Henry Knox, continued; Timothy Pickering, of Massachusetts, appointed January 2d, 1795; James McHenry, of Maryland, appointed January 27th, 1796.

Attorneys-General.—Edmund Randolph, of Virginia, continued; William Bradford, of Pennsylvania, appointed January 28th, 1794; Charles Lee, of Virginia, appointed December 10th, 1795.

CHAPTER III.

CAMPAIGN OF 1796.

FEDERAL NOMINEES.

For President.
JOHN ADAMS of Massachusetts.

For Vice-President.
THOMAS PINCKNEY of South Carolina.

REPUBLICAN NOMINEES.

For President.
THOMAS JEFFERSON of Virginia.

For Vice-President.
AARON BURR of New York.

CAUCUSES AND NOMINATIONS.

WASHINGTON's memorable farewell address, issued to the people September 17th, 1796, assured them that he would retire from public life at the end of his term.

No other man in the nation could command its almost unanimous support; and when, therefore, the last hope of his continuing the executive head of the Government for another four years had been dispelled, the two great parties engaged in a struggle for ascendency, which, although the first party contest, was conducted in a manner seemingly so modern, that he who traces the history of party warfare will discover that little change has been made in the weapons which were then forged and those now used in political strife.

WENDELL PHILLIPS.

At caucuses held in Philadelphia, the candidates nominated by the Federalists for President and Vice-President were John Adams and Thomas Pinckney ; on the part of the Republicans Thomas Jefferson and Aaron Burr were presented.

The election, which occurred in the autumn, was a close one ; but the system of choosing a President and Vice-President which obtained from 1789 to 1804 gave a victory to both parties. Mr. Adams, receiving the highest number of electoral votes, was declared President, and Mr. Jefferson, receiving the next highest number, was chosen Vice-President.

AARON BURR.

Aaron Burr, the third Vice-President of the United States, was born in Newark, New Jersey, on the 5th of February, 1756.

His father, Aaron Burr, was the learned and devout president of Princeton College, and one of its principal founders.

Both of Burr's parents died before he had reached the age of three years, and to this early deprivation of the precept and example of his exemplary parents may be attributed his erratic and immoral life. He entered Princeton College at the age of twelve, and graduated at sixteen, having won for himself, during his college career, the reputation of a youth of fine natural parts and studious application. While in his twentieth year, before he had completed his preparation for the bar, to which he had determined to devote himself, he joined the American army under Washington, at Cambridge, in 1775, as a private, and accompanied Arnold in the expedition to Canada, and was present at the attack on Quebec. For his services in this campaign he was made major, and invited to join the military family of Washington. Some event soon occurred which compelled Burr to leave headquarters, and produced in the mind of Washington an impression against him, which was never removed. As aide-de-camp to General Putnam, Burr was engaged in the defence of New York, and in 1777 he was made lieutenant-colonel, with the command of his regiment. He was in the camp at Valley Forge, and distinguished himself at the battle of Monmouth, where he commanded a brigade. During the winter of 1778-79 he was stationed in Westchester County, New York, and for a short time was in command at West Point.

Early in the following spring he resigned his commission, because he affected to despise the military talents of Washington. In 1782 he completed his legal course of study, and was admitted to the bar at Albany; and in July of the same year he married Mrs. Prevost, the widow of a British officer who had died in the West Indies. In 1783 he entered upon the practice of his profession in the city of New York. The following year he was elected to the State Legislature, and five years later was appointed attorney-general of the State.

In 1791 he was chosen United States Senator, and while in the Senate he was recommended for the mission to France; but Washington discerned qualities in him which he believed were unfit for a representative to that country to possess, and he refused to appoint him. Failing of a re-election to the United States Senate in 1797, he accepted another term in the State Legislature. In 1800 he was an active participant in the Presidential canvass, and to his efforts may be attributed the success of the Republicans in New York, upon the action of which State, at the beginning of the century, as now, the result of the Presidential election is thought to depend.

On account of the prominence he thus obtained, the friends of Mr. Jefferson brought him forward for the Vice-Presidency. An equal number of votes having been cast for Jefferson and Burr in the electoral college, the election of a President devolved upon the House of Representatives, most of the Federal members voting for Burr. After a contest of several days Jefferson was elected President, and, in accordance with the provisions of the Constitution at that time, Burr became Vice-President. His conduct in permitting himself to be used by his political opponents, the Federalists, in order to defeat the candidate of his party, and whom he himself had supported, dissolved his connection with the Republicans, and destroyed his political influence. The Federalists nominated him for Governor of New York in 1804, but many of the leaders of that party refused to support him, and he was defeated. That bitter contest for the governorship led to the duel between Burr and Alexander Hamilton on the 11th of July, 1804, in which the latter was killed. For this act Burr was disfranchised by the laws of New York, and was indicted for murder in New Jersey. His term as Vice-President closed on the 4th of March, 1805, and in April following he set out upon his mysterious Western journey. What were his real schemes is uncertain, and perhaps they were as indefinite in his own mind as they were anomalous to others; but they seem to have included the formation of a new government in the South, on the borders of and perhaps partly within the United States. He purchased four hundred thousand acres of land on the Red River, and gave his adherents to understand that the Spanish dominions were to be conquered. His proceedings excited so much alarm that on the 27th of November, 1806, President Jefferson issued a proclamation against him.

While endeavoring to make his way to the coast he was arrested in Alabama, February 19th, 1807, and brought to Richmond, Virginia, for trial, upon an indictment for high treason. The trial began on the 27th of March, and lasted very nearly six months. No overt act of treason could be proved, and the jury brought in the verdict, "Aaron Burr is not proved to be guilty under the indictment by any evidence submitted to us." He was accordingly set at liberty, and in 1808 went to Europe, hoping to obtain means to effect his designs, which had now taken the form of an attempt on Mexico. In this he was disappointed, and after living abroad for some years, a part of the time in great poverty, he returned to America in 1812, and resumed the practice of law in New York ; and while his talents brought him considerable business, he never regained the position which he had formerly held at the bar. In the seventy-eighth year of his age he married Madame Jumel, a wealthy widow, but was shortly afterward divorced, and died neglected on the 14th of September, 1836. He was an accomplished and skilful lawyer and an eloquent and effective speaker.

PRESIDENT JOHN ADAM'S CABINET.

Secretaries of State.—Timothy Pickering, of Massachusetts, continued : John Marshall, of Virginia, appointed May 13th, 1800.

Secretaries of the Treasury.—Oliver Wolcott, of Connecticut, continued : Samuel Dexter, of Massachusetts, appointed January 1st, 1801.

Secretaries of War.—James McHenry, of Maryland, continued ; Samuel Dexter, of Massachusetts, appointed May 13th, 1800.

Secretaries of the Navy.—George Cabot, of Massachusetts, appointed May 3d, 1798 ; Benjamin Stoddard, of Maryland, appointed May 21st, 1798.

Attorney-General.—Charles Lee, of Virginia, appointed March 4th, 1797.

CHAPTER IV.

CAMPAIGN OF 1800.

REPUBLICAN NOMINEES.

For President.
THOMAS JEFFERSON of Virginia.

For Vice-President.
AARON BURR of New York.

FEDERAL NOMINEES.

For President.
JOHN ADAMS of Massachusetts.

For Vice-President.
CHARLES C. PINCKNEY of South Carolina.

CAUCUSES AND NOMINATIONS.

At a Republican Congressional caucus, held at Philadelphia to nominate candidates for the fourth Presidential term, Thomas Jefferson was placed at the head of the ticket, and Aaron Burr second. The Federalists at their caucus, held in the same city, gave Adams a nomination for re-election, and Charles C. Pinckney was nominated for Vice-President.

The vote for Jefferson and Burr being equal, there was no choice for President by the electoral votes. On the 11th of February, 1801, the House of Representatives proceeded to the election of a President. On the first ballot eight States voted for Jefferson, six for Burr, and the votes of two were divided.

Balloting continued without a choice until the 17th, when on the thirty-sixth ballot ten States voted for Jefferson, four for Burr, and two in blank. Thomas Jefferson was thus elected President and Aaron Burr Vice-President.

ALEXANDER HAMILTON.

Alexander Hamilton was born in the island of Nevis, West Indies, on the 11th of January, 1757. Hamilton's father failed in business, and passed the remainder of his life in poverty. His mother died in his childhood, but relatives of hers, who resided at Santa Cruz, took charge of the orphan, her only surviving child. There were but meagre advantages of education at Santa Cruz; but possessing the French as well as the English tongue, young Hamilton eagerly read such books in both languages as fell in his way. At the age of twelve he was placed in the counting-house of a merchant at Santa Cruz; but this occupation was not to his taste, and he spoke with disgust of the "grovelling condition of a clerk," and wished for a war. Notwithstanding his aversion to his employment, he applied himself to it with characteristic assiduity; and the practical knowledge which he thus acquired was doubtless a stepping-stone to the remarkable ability which he subsequently acquired as a financier.

He began to write early, and a description of a hurricane which visited St. Christopher in 1772 was so vividly described by his pen that it excited so much attention as to induce his friends to comply with his wish and send him to New York to be educated. On reaching this country he was placed in a grammar school at Elizabethtown, New Jersey, and after a few months he entered King's (now Columbia) College. Besides the regular studies of an undergraduate, he attended lectures on anatomy, with the idea of becoming a physician. While he was thus engaged the war of the Revolution was inaugurated.

On July 6th, 1774, he attended a public meeting in New York, and made a speech, which attracted attention to him. Shortly after, this he became a correspondent of *Holt's Journal*, the organ of the New York patriots. A pamphlet having appeared attacking the proceedings of the Continental Congress, Hamilton replied to it in another pamphlet, written with so much ability that its authorship was ascribed to Jay. This reply drew out an answer, to which Hamilton rejoined in a second pamphlet. These pamphlets, and another which he published in June, 1775, on the "Quebec Bill," gave him standing and consideration among the popular leaders. Meanwhile he had joined a volunteer corps, and applied himself to obtain information and instruction as an artillerist. In March, 1776, though yet but nineteen years of age, he obtained, on the recommendation of General Schuyler, then in command of the Northern Department, a commission as captain in a company raised by the State of New York. He led the fortunes of his brave band in all the principal engagements, until it was reduced to twenty-five men. The spirit and ability of the young captain had not escaped notice. He had received invitations from two major-generals to take a place in their staff, which he declined; but he accepted a similar offer from Washington on the 1st of March, 1777, with the rank of lieutenant-colonel. In 1780 a rebuke from Washington, which he thought unmerited, was answered on the spot by a resignation of his position as a member of Washington's staff, which he declined to withdraw, though Washington sent him an apology. But this separation did not interrupt their mutual confidence and esteem.

In 1781 he began the study of law at Albany, and after a few months he obtained a license to practise. A few days later he was elected by the Legislature of New York a delegate to the Continental Congress, and took his seat in November, 1782. This he resigned when the British evacuated New York, and removed thither and commenced the practice of his profession. An act had been passed by the Legislature just before, which was a very opportune provision in its benefits to young lawyers admitted at that time, disqualifying, as it did, all attorneys and counsellors from practice who could not produce satisfactory certificates of attachment to Whig principles. Most or all the old city lawyers fell within this prohibition, which remained in force for three or four years, and enabled Hamilton and other young advocates to immediately acquire a practice which otherwise they might have waited years. Hamilton immediately distinguished himself at the bar. He was one of the founders of the Manumission Society, the object of which was the abolition of slavery then existing in the State of New York. By appointment of the State Legislature he attended, in 1786, the convention at Annapolis, and as a member of it drafted the address to the States which led to the convention the next year by which the Federal Constitution was framed. On October 27th, 1787, there appeared in a New York journal the first number of a series of papers entitled "The Federalist," in support of the Constitution against the various objections urged to it. These papers continued till the following June, reaching the number of eighty-five, and were republished throughout the States, and made a strong impression in favor of the new scheme of government. Sixty-five of these papers were written by Hamilton, and the balance by Jay and Madison. They are still read and quoted as a standard commentary on the ends and aims of the Federal Constitution and its true interpretation. The Government having been put into operation under it, and Congress at its first session having passed acts reorganizing the executive departments, Washington, in 1789, selected Hamilton as Secretary of the Treasury. This office he resigned after six years' service, and resumed the practice of law in New York. He still remained, however, a warm supporter of Washington's administration. In the preparation of Washington's "Farewell Address" Hamilton's assistance was asked and given, precisely to what extent has been and still is a matter of controversy. In the summer of 1798 Washington was appointed commander-in-chief, with the title of lieutenant-general. He accepted, on the condition that he should not be called into active service and that Hamilton should be major-general, thus throwing upon him the details of the organization of the army. On the death of Washington, December 14th, 1799, Hamilton succeeded to the command-in-chief, but shortly afterward resigned his commission and again resumed the practice of law. This was the last public trust which he held, but he exerted a potent influence on the politics of the nation until his death, which occurred in New York on the 12th of July, 1804, from a mortal wound received at the hands of Aaron Burr in a duel which occurred the day before at Weehawken, on the Hudson River, opposite the city of New York.

Hamilton enjoyed among his contemporaries, both friends and foes, a reputation for extraordinary ability. He excelled equally as a writer and speaker, and his influence over men was no less marked.

Mr. Van Buren says: "That the policy of every administration of the Federal Government for the first twelve years of its existence was shaped, and the action of the Federal party guided by the opinions and advice of Hamilton, was the general impression of the opponents of that party, and of course known to the leading Federalists. In all my conversations with Mr. Jefferson, when he spoke of the course pursued by the Federal party, invariably personified it by saying 'Hamilton' did or insisted thus; and, on the other hand, 'the Republicans' held or claimed so and so; and that upon my calling his attention to the peculiarity of his expression, he smiled, and attributed his habit to the universal conviction of the Republicans that Hamilton directed everything."

PRESIDENT JEFFERSON'S FIRST CABINET.

Secretary of State.—James Madison, of Virginia, appointed March 5th, 1801.

Secretary of the Treasury.—Albert Gallatin, of Pennsylvania, appointed May 14th, 1801.

Secretary of War.—Henry Dearborn, of Massachusetts, appointed March 5th, 1801.

Secretaries of the Navy.—Benjamin Stoddard, of Maryland, appointed March 5th, 1801 ; Robert Smith, of Maryland, appointed July 15th, 1801 ; Jacob Crowninshield, of Massachusetts, appointed March 2d, 1805.

Attorneys-General.—Levi Lincoln, of Massachusetts, appointed March 5th, 1801 ; Robert Smith, of Maryland, appointed March 2d, 1805.

CHAPTER V.

CAMPAIGN OF 1804

REPUBLICAN NOMINEES.

For President.
THOMAS JEFFERSON of Virginia.

For Vice-President.
GEORGE CLINTON of New York.

FEDERAL NOMINEES.

For President.
CHARLES C. PINCKNEY of South Carolina.

For Vice-President.
RUFUS KING of New York.

CAUCUSES AND NOMINATIONS.

CAUCUSES, composed of Congressmen, were held by both parties in the city of Philadelphia.

Thomas Jefferson was nominated by the Republicans for President, and George Clinton was placed on the ticket for the office of Vice-President.

The Federalists nominated Charles C. Pinckney and Rufus King for the two highest offices.

Jefferson's administration had been so popular that his re-election was assured, and no contest was made. The canvass was uneventful, and the election resulted in Jefferson's re-election by 162 out of 176 electoral votes.

The electoral count for Vice-President gave Clinton the same number.

No platforms were adopted by either party.

JOHN ADAMS.

John Adams was born in Braintree, Massachusetts, on October 19th, 1735. He graduated at Harvard College in 1755, and while he was preparing himself for the profession of law taught school at Worcester for two years. He was admitted to the bar in 1758, and afterward resided with his father at Braintree for several years. John Adams was pre-eminently gifted as an orator. With a clear and sonorous voice, a sound constitution, a quick conception, a discriminating judgment, and a ready delivery, he soon won laurels as a lawyer and an orator. In 1761 his patriotic zeal was inflamed by the arguments of James Otis on the subject of writs of assistance. He married, in 1764, Abigail Smith, a woman in every way worthy of him. The passage of the Stamp Act, in 1765, was the first occasion of his active participation in political affairs. He was offered the position of Advocate-General in 1763 by the Tory party, which he declined. He removed to Boston in 1768, and soon obtained an extensive practice. He was elected a member of the Massachusetts Legislature in 1770. Mr. Adams was one of the five delegates sent by Massachusetts to the first Continental Congress in Philadelphia, in 1774. To a friend who urged him not to engage in the perilous enterprise of revolution, Mr. Adams said: "The die is now cast. I have crossed the Rubicon. Sink or swim, live or die, survive or perish with my country is my unalterable determination."

In Congress he found a fitting arena for the exercise of those great talents, both of business and debate, which ultimately raised him to the leadership of that body. He was the first to propose George Washington as the Commander-in-Chief of the army. He was again elected to the Federal Congress, and went to Philadelphia in February, 1776. Soon afterward he said: "All our troubles and misfortunes arise from the reluctance of the Southern colonies to Republican government." On the 7th of June, 1776, he seconded the resolution of Richard Henry Lee, declaring "that these colonies are, and of right ought to be, free and independent States." Mr. Adams made a memorable speech on the subject on July 2d, in reference to which Thomas Jefferson wrote: "John Adams was the ablest advocate and champion of independence on the floor of the House. His power of thought and expression moved his hearers from their seats."

Mr. Adams was chairman of the Board of War appointed in June, 1776. He went to France as Commissioner of the United States in 1777, and remained in Paris two years. He was Minister at London from 1785 to 1788. When, in 1789, Washington was inaugurated as President John Adams became Vice-President. He was again elected Vice-President in 1792. Adams was elected President in 1796, but was defeated in 1800 by Thomas Jefferson. Having lived to see his son, John Quincy Adams, elected President, he died at Quincy, Massachusetts, on the 4th of July, 1826.

The resolution of July 2d, 1776, which resulted in the framing of the Declaration of Independence, was to Mr. Adams a source of peculiar pleasure. The transport of his feelings may be seen vividly portrayed in the letter which he wrote to Mrs. Adams the succeeding day.

"Yesterday," he says, "the greatest question was decided that was ever debated in America, and greater, perhaps, never was or will be decided among men. A resolution was passed, without one dissenting colony, 'that these United States are, and of right ought to be, free and independent States.' The day is passed. The 4th of July, 1776, will be a memorable epoch in the history of America. I am apt to believe it will be celebrated by succeeding generations as the great anniversary festival. It ought to be commemorated, as the day of deliverance, by solemn acts of devotion to Almighty God. It ought to be solemnized with pomps, shows, games, sports, guns, bells, bonfires, and illuminations, from one end of the continent to the other, from this time forward forever. You will think me transported with enthusiasm, but I am not. I am well aware of the toil and blood and treasure that it will cost to maintain this declaration, and support and defend these States ; yet, through all the gloom, I can see the rays of light and glory. I can see that the end is worth more than all the means, and that posterity will triumph."

"Verily, there were prophets and seers in those days !"

Mr. Adams's reply to Lord Howe will ever be remembered. "Sir," he said, "you may view me in any light you please, except in that of a British subject."

Mr. Adams had not, until a few days previous, shown indications of rapidly failing strength. The 4th of July, 1826, found him unable to rise from his bed. He was not, however, aware of so near an approach of death. On being asked to suggest a toast for the customary celebration of the day, he exclaimed, "Independence forever !" These were his last coherent words.

It is known that the illustrious Jefferson departed a few hours before him, and we cannot close this imperfect sketch more appropriately than by borrowing the language of one who most deeply felt the impressiveness of this solemn and memorable event.

"They departed, cheered by the benedictions of their country, to whom they left the inheritance of their fame and the memory of their bright example. . . . At the last, extended on a bed of death, with but sense and sensibility left to breathe a last aspiration to heaven of blessing upon their country."

PRESIDENT JEFFERSON'S SECOND CABINET.

Secretary of State.—James Madison, of Virginia, continued.
Secretary of the Treasury.—Albert Gallatin, of Pennsylvania, continued.
Secretary of War.—Henry Dearborn, of Massachusetts, continued.
Secretary of the Navy.—Jacob Crowninshield, of Massachusetts, continued.
Attorneys-General.—Robert Smith, of Maryland, continued; John Breckinridge, of Kentucky, appointed December 25th, 1805; Cæsar A. Rodney, of Delaware, appointed January 20th, 1807.

HENRY WARD BEECHER.

CHAPTER VI.

CAMPAIGN OF 1808.

REPUBLICAN NOMINEES.

For President.
JAMES MADISON of Virginia.

For Vice-President.
GEORGE CLINTON of New York.

FEDERAL NOMINEES.

For President.
CHARLES C. PINCKNEY of South Carolina.

For Vice-President.
RUFUS KING of New York.

CAUCUSES AND NOMINATIONS.

In January, 1808, when Mr. Jefferson's second term was about to close, a Republican Congressional caucus was held at Washington to decide as to the relative claims of Madison and Monroe for the succession, the Legislature of Virginia, which had been said to exert a potent influence over such questions, being, on this occasion, unable to agree as to which of her favored sons should have the preference. Ninety-four out of the one hundred and thirty-six Republican members of Congress attended this caucus, and declared their preference of Madison, who received eighty-three votes, the remaining being divided between Monroe and George Clinton.

Madison's nomination met with bitter opposition from a wing of the party, headed by John Randolph, and James Monroe was nominated by this dissenting element.

Charles C. Pinckney and Rufus King were again placed in nomination by the Federalists. A vigorous canvass followed these nominations, owing to the break in the Republican ranks. During the campaign Clinton was suggested as a proper man to unite the contending forces in his party. These differences between the Republicans operated to strengthen the opposition party; but the dominant party was too strong to be overthrown by even its own bitter discord, and Madison was elected by a large majority.

JOHN RANDOLPH.

One of the most remarkable men that ever lived was John Randolph, of Roanoke. He was born on the 2d of June, 1773, near Petersburg, Virginia. In his veins were blended the aristocratic blood of England and the blood royal of primitive America. His lordly bearing, aboriginal descent, eccentric career, and extraordinary eloquence early fastened the attention of his countrymen upon him, and through many years engrossed popular regard to a wonderful degree. John Randolph's early education, according to his own account, was very irregular. In the year 1788 he was sent to college in New York, but returned to Virginia in 1790. In the same year he went to Philadelphia to study law in the office of Edmund Randolph, then Attorney-General of the United States. But his law studies scarcely extended beyond the first book of Blackstone. He became of age in June, 1794, up to which time he appears to have led an irregular, desultory life, with a residence as fluctuating as his object of pursuit was undecided. Randolph made his first appearance in public life in 1799, as a candidate for Congress, and was elected. He was indebted to his eloquence for success in this early contest, as he was without family influence in the district, and was a mere boy in appearance. His opponent was the veteran statesman and famous orator, Patrick Henry. The exciting questions which arose out of Mr. Madison's resolutions of 1798 were the chief matter in debate during the canvass.

An anecdote has been preserved strongly characteristic of both combatants. Randolph was addressing the populace in answer to Mr. Henry, when a companion said to the latter, "Come, Henry, let us go; it is not worth while to listen to *that boy*." "Stay, my friend," replied the sagacious patriot, "there is an old man's head on that boy's shoulders."

When he entered Congress his youthful aspect, among other striking traits, attracted universal surprise. When he presented himself at the clerk's table to qualify, the official demanded his age. "Ask my constituents," was the characteristic reply. Mr. Randolph soon became a marked man in the national councils. His fearless thought, pungent language, withering sarcasm, and general power as a prompt and passionate debater attracted the Administration as well as excited the dread of all parties within Congress and without. A pen picture at one time described his person as follows : "John Randolph is about six feet high. He has elevated shoulders, a small head, and a physiognomy, all the parts of which are entirely unintellectual except his eye. His hair is dark, thin, and lank, and lays close to his head. His voice is as shrill as a fife, but its clear, shrieking tones can be distinctly heard by a large audience. The muscles and skin about his face are shrivelled and cadaverous, like wrinkled parchment. His lips are thin, compressed, and colorless. Tall as he looks, his weight is not more than one hundred and thirty pounds." Of the new Constitution of Virginia, he said : "It was brought into life with the *sardonic* grin of death upon its countenance." In that expression the outline and tone of his own portrait may be traced. His language was pointed and severe, full of condensed fire and inhuman energy. His oratory was Spartan brevity and force ; his words fell like vipers among his hearers, and stung them into fiery excitement. He was morbid and morose to excess, but his gloom was volcanic heat, ready to explode at any moment and in any direction. Suddenly his stoical nature would become irrepressible. and his cold, sinister eye blazed with splendid fires, and radiated from his hueless face like a wintry sky flashing with electric bolts.

A political opponent boasted on the stump that if his mind was not naturally as strong as that of the orator of Roanoke, he had done his best, by an arduous collegiate course, to improve it. "Not the first weak soil. gentlemen," exclaimed Randolph, interrupting him, "that excessive cultivation has reduced to barrenness."

John Randolph at one time was regarded, and perhaps still is by some persons, as the prince of American orators. Viewing his merits in the light of his public deeds, we think that if an apotheosis is to be granted him at all, it should be in company with such men as Warren Hastings.

PRESIDENT MADISON'S FIRST CABINET.

Secretaries of State.—Robert Smith, of Maryland, appointed March 6th, 1809; James Monroe, of Virginia, appointed April 2d, 1811.

Secretary of the Treasury.—Albert Gallatin, of Pennsylvania, continued.

Secretaries of War.—William Eustis, of Massachusetts, appointed March 7th, 1809; John Armstrong, of New York, appointed January 13th, 1813.

Secretaries of the Navy.—Paul Hamilton, of South Carolina, appointed March 7th, 1809; William Jones, of Pennsylvania, appointed January 12th, 1813.

Attorneys-General.—Cæsar A. Rodney, of Delaware, continued; William Pinkney, of Maryland, appointed December 11th, 1811.

CHAPTER VII.

CAMPAIGN OF 1812.

REGULAR REPUBLICAN NOMINEES.

For President.
JAMES MADISON of Virginia.

For Vice-President.
ELBRIDGE GERRY of Massachusetts.

REPUBLICAN NOMINEES, SUPPORTED BY THE FEDERAL PARTY.

For President.
DE WITT CLINTON of New York.

For Vice-President.
JARED INGERSOLL of Pennsylvania.

CAUCUSES AND NOMINATIONS.

IN 1812 the Republican party, which was then in power, was divided on the question of war with England. The leaders of the war element were Henry Clay and John C. Calhoun.

Madison's known sympathy was with the opposition; but these leaders refused him that support which he knew was necessary to secure a second term, unless he identified himself with the war element. He yielded to their persuasion, and was nominated for re-election at a Republican Congressional caucus, held at Washington on the 8th of May.

De Witt Clinton, a prominent candidate before the Washington caucus, returned to New York with his disappointment, and the Republican members of the Legislature gratified him with a nomination for the Presidency on the 17th of August.

The Federalists made no nominations, and indirectly gave their support to Clinton and Ingersoll.

The electoral votes were counted on the 8th day of February, 1813, and were found to be, for President, one hundred and twenty-eight for Madison and eighty-nine for Clinton ; for Vice-President, Gerry one hundred and thirty-one and eighty-six for Ingersoll. Madison and Gerry were therefore declared elected.

HENRY CLAY.

Henry Clay, the great statesman and orator, was born on the 12th of April, 1777, in Hanover County, Virginia, not far from the birthplace and home of Patrick Henry.

At the age of fifteen Mr. Clay entered the office of the clerk of the High Court of Chancery. Four years later he commenced the study of law, and was admitted to practice when he had attained his twentieth year.

In November, 1797, he removed to Lexington, Kentucky, where he established himself in the profession of the law. In a speech made at his home, June 9th, 1842, he said of his early experience : " In looking back upon my origin and progress through life, I have great reason to be thankful. My father died in 1781, leaving me an infant of too tender years to retain any recollection of his smiles or endearments. My surviving parent removed to this State in 1792, leaving me, a boy of fifteen years of age, in the office of the High Court of Chancery, in the City of Richmond, without guardian, without pecuniary support, to steer my course as I might or could. A neglected education was improved by my own irregular exertions, without the benefit of systematic instruction. I studied law principally in the office of a lamented friend, the late Governor Brooke, then Attorney-General of Virginia, and also under the auspices of the venerable and lamented Chancellor Wythe, for whom I had acted as an amanuensis. I obtained a license to practise the profession from the judges of the Court of Appeals, of Virginia, and established myself in Lexington in 1797, without patrons, without the favor or countenance of the great or opulent, without the means of paying my weekly board, and in the midst of a bar uncommonly distinguished by eminent members. I remember how comfortable I thought I should be if I could make £100 Virginia money per year, and with what delight I received the first fifteen-shilling fee. My hopes were more than realized. I immediately rushed into a successful and lucrative practice."

In 1803 Mr. Clay was elected to the Legislature ; in 1806 he was chosen to the Senate of the United States to fill a vacancy. After the expiration of his term in the Senate he was re-elected to the State Legislature and chosen Speaker of that body, which office he held until 1809, when he was again elected to the Senate of the United States to fill another vacancy. From the first he took a prominent part in the discussion of the leading questions before Congress, and came forward as an ardent advocate of internal improvement, of domestic manufactures, and of a protective policy. The eloquent defence of such public measures has given the orator of Ashland a distinction second to no American statesman.

When his Senatorial term again expired, Mr. Clay was immediately elected to the House of Representatives, and took his seat on the 4th of November, 1811. On the first day of the session he was chosen Speaker by a triumphant vote—an honor which had never before been conferred upon a new member. This station he held, with the exception of two short intervals, until 1825.

Mr. Clay entered Congress just before the last conflict with Great Britain. That nation had committed a long series of outrages on our Government by harassing our commerce, searching our vessels, and impressing our seamen. Such injuries could be no longer endured by Americans, and war was declared against Great Britain, June 18th, 1812. Mr. Clay urged this declaration with "almost as much vehemence and pertinacity as Cato the destruction of Carthage."

When the war had commenced, Mr. Clay exerted all his burning eloquence for its vigorous prosecution. In one of the most powerful speeches he ever made—that "On the New Army Bill," delivered in the House January 8th, 1813—he said, with the enthusiasm of a patriot and with the eloquence of Demosthenes : "My plan would be to call out the ample resources of the country, give them a judicious direction, prosecute the war with the utmost vigor, strike wherever we can reach the enemy, at sea or on land, and negotiate the terms of a peace at Quebec or at Halifax. We are told that England is a proud and lofty nation, which, disdaining to wait for danger, meets it half way. Haughty as she is, we once triumphed over her ; and, if we do not listen to the counsels of timidity and despair, we shall again prevail. In such a cause, with the aid of Providence, we must come out crowned with success; but if we fail, let us fail like men—lash ourselves to our gallant tars, and expire together in one common struggle, fighting for *Free Trade and Seamen's Rights!*"

Mr. Clay was one of the most influential, popular, and eloquent speakers ever chosen by the House of Representatives. He presided over the deliberations of that body with great ability and sagacity. "Undoubtedly," says a writer, "at this time, even in his youthful age, he had no rival in popularity. His name was everywhere familiar as 'household words.'"

At the commencement of the year 1814, Mr. Clay was appointed one of the commissioners to negotiate a treaty of peace with Great Britain; and on the 19th of January he resigned his station as Speaker of the House in a very impressive address. Mr. Clay took a leading part in the negotiations of the Treaty of Ghent. Before his return home he visited several portions of Europe, and was received everywhere with marked attention. On his return to the United States he was greeted with the greatest enthusiasm, and unanimously re-elected to Congress. On taking his seat, in December, 1815, he was again triumphantly chosen Speaker of the House. His popularity in the country had reached a lofty height. Peace with Great Britain had been satisfactorily arranged, and largely through his instrumentality; and the multitude lavished upon him every expression of grateful feeling and personal devotion. He was properly associated in their minds with the national glory and national prosperity.

In 1825 Mr. Clay was appointed Secretary of State by President John Quincy Adams. This office he relinquished at the close of Mr. Adams's administration, and after remaining two years in retirement, he was elected to the United States Senate in 1831.

It would exceed our narrow limits to follow Mr. Clay through his brilliant Senatorial career. The distinguished services which he rendered his country in that body will ever emblazon the pages of the nation's history with a radiance which the brightest effulgence of his gifted contemporaries cannot dim. On the 31st of March, 1842, Mr. Clay resigned his seat in the Senate. When it was known that he was to deliver his farewell address, a large audience filled the Senate Chamber.

It was an interesting and solemn occasion. Mr. Clay addressed the Senate in a most affecting speech, from which the following beautiful extracts are taken:

"Full of attraction, however, as a seat in the Senate is, sufficient as it is to satisfy the aspirations of the most ambitious heart, I have long determined to relinquish it, and to seek that repose which can be enjoyed only in the shades of private life, in the circle of one's own family, and in the tranquil enjoyments included in one enchanting word—*home*."

He paid the following glowing tribute to the State of Kentucky : " But scarce had I set my foot upon her generous soil when I was embraced with parental fondness, caressed as though I had been a favorite child, and patronized with liberal and unbounded munificence. From that period the highest honors of the State have been freely bestowed upon me ; and when in the darkest hour of calumny and detraction I seemed to be assailed by all the rest of the world, she interposed her broad and impenetrable shield, repelled the poisonous shafts that were aimed for my destruction, and vindicated my good name from every malignant and unfounded aspersion. I return with indescribable pleasure to linger a while longer and mingle with the warm-hearted and whole-souled people of that State ; and when the last scene shall forever close upon me, I hope my earthly remains will be laid under her green sod with those of her gallant and patriotic sons."

Leaving the Senate, Mr. Clay retired to private life. In 1844 he was the Whig candidate for the Presidency, but was defeated by the election of James K. Polk. In December, 1848, Mr. Clay was again elected to the United States Senate by a unanimous vote. He died at his post of duty, in the city of Washington, on the 29th of June, 1852, in the seventy-sixth year of his age, lamented by an admiring nation.

PRESIDENT MADISON'S SECOND CABINET.

Secretary of State.—James Monroe, of Virginia, continued.

Secretaries of the Treasury.—Albert Gallatin, of Pennsylvania, continued ; George W. Campbell, of Tennessee, appointed February 9th, 1814 ; Alexander I. Dallas, of Pennsylvania, appointed October 6th, 1814.

Secretaries of War.—John Armstrong, of New York, continued ; James Monroe, of Virginia, appointed September 26th, 1814 ; William H. Crawford, of Georgia, appointed March 3d, 1815.

Secretaries of the Navy.—William Jones, of Pennsylvania, continued ; Benjamin W. Crowninshield, of Massachusetts, appointed December 19th, 1814.

Attorneys-General.—William Pinkney, of Maryland, continued ; Richard Rush, of Pennsylvania, appointed February 10th, 1814.

CHAPTER VIII.

CAMPAIGN OF 1816.

REPUBLICAN NOMINEES.

For President.
JAMES MONROE of Virginia.

For Vice-President.
DANIEL D. TOMPKINS of New York.

FEDERAL NOMINEES.

For President.
RUFUS KING of New York.

For Vice-President.
JOHN E. HOWARD of Maryland.

CAUCUSES AND NOMINATIONS.

THE objections which had repeatedly been made against the caucus system of Presidential nominations broke out with renewed vigor in a caucus held at Philadelphia on the 16th of March, and two unsuccessful attempts were made to pass a resolution declaring it inexpedient to make caucus nominations by members of Congress. The practice had previously caused much dissatisfaction, and at this meeting nineteen of the Congressmen refused to take part in the proceedings.

Monroe and Tompkins, however, were nominated for the offices of President and Vice-President by a vote which was declared unanimous.

At the same time the objection to what was called the "Virginia Dynasty" was renewed, and the overdrafts made on that State for national rulers was criticised by all classes who were imbued with State pride.

CAMPAIGN OF 1816.

The Federal party nominated Rufus King and John E. Howard. They were joined by the Clintonians, who repudiated caucus nominations; but this coalition developed little strength, and the Monroe ticket was elected by one hundred and eighty-three electoral votes against thirty-four for King.

MARTIN VAN BUREN.

Martin Van Buren, one of the most sagacious of American politicians, was born at Kinderhook, New York, on the 5th of December, 1782. He began the study of law at the age of fourteen, and passed the last year of his studies in the office of Hon. W. P. Van Ness, in the city of New York. At the age of eighteen he was a delegate in a nominating convention of the Republican party. In 1808 he was appointed surrogate of Columbia County, and in 1812 he was elected to the State Senate, and in that body voted for electors pledged to support De Witt Clinton for the Presidency. In 1815 he was elected attorney-general of the State, which office he held until 1819. In 1816 he was again a member of the Senate, holding the two offices together.

In 1818 Mr. Van Buren set on foot a new organization of the Democratic party in his State, and became the ruling spirit of a coterie of able politicians, known as the Albany regency, among whom B. F. Butler and W. L. Marcy were prominent, who held the political control of the State uninterruptedly for more than twenty years. In 1821 Mr. Van Buren was elected to a seat in the United States Senate, and was also elected a member of the convention to revise the State Constitution.

In the latter body he advocated an extension of the elective franchise, but opposed universal suffrage. He voted against depriving colored citizens of the franchise, but supported the proposal to require of them a freehold qualification of two hundred and fifty dollars. In 1827 he was re-elected to the Senate, but resigned that office on being elected Governor of New York in 1828. As governor he proposed the safety fund banking system adopted by the Legislature in 1829. In March, 1829, he was invited to a seat in President Jackson's Cabinet and given the office of Secretary of State, which office he resigned on April 7th, 1831. He was subsequently appointed Minister to England, and reached that country in

September; but his nomination to that office, submitted to the Senate in December, was rejected on the ground that while Secretary of State he had instructed the United States Minister to England to beg from that country, as a favor, certain concessions in regard to trade with her colonies in the West Indies, which he should have demanded as a right; and that he had carried our domestic party contests and their results into foreign diplomatic negotiations. The friends and admirers of Mr. Van Buren, to recompense him for his humiliating trip to England, nominated him, on the 22d of May, 1832, for the Vice-Presidency, on the ticket with General Jackson for re-election to the Presidency; and in the subsequent election Mr. Van Buren again came into office. The Democratic National Convention, which met at Baltimore on the 20th of May, 1835, unanimously nominated him for President. The election in November, 1836, gave him a large majority over his competitors, General Harrison and Daniel Webster.

The country, which for some time had felt a pecuniary embarrassment, after his inauguration, on the 4th of March, 1837, became involved in a crisis of unprecedented severity. Commerce and manufactures were prostrate; hundreds of wealthy mercantile houses in every section were bankrupt; imposing public meetings attributed these disasters to the policy of the Government, and two months after Mr. Van Buren's inauguration the crash was consummated by the universal suspension of specie payments by the banks. On the 15th of May he summoned an extraordinary session of Congress to meet the following September. Mr. Van Buren, in his special message, advised that a bankrupt law for banking and other corporations should be enacted, and that the approaching deficit in the treasury be made good by withholding from the States the fourth and last instalment of a previous large surplus ordered to be deposited with them by the act of June, 1836, and by the temporary issue of six million dollars of treasury notes.

An insurrectionary movement begun in Canada, in the latter part of 1837, having found aid and sympathy within our borders, Mr. Van Buren issued two proclamations, enjoining all citizens to refrain from violating the laws and the treaties of the country, and he sent General Scott to preserve the peace there. It was during Mr. Van Buren's administration that the agitation of the slavery question was temporarily stopped in the House of Representatives. Mr. Slade, of Vermont, introduced the subject in a long and elaborate anti-slavery speech, whereupon the Southern members withdrew for separate deliberation, and Mr. Rhett, of South Carolina, proposed to

FREDERICK DOUGLASS.

declare that it was expedient that the Union should be dissolved ; but on motion of Mr. Patten, of Virginia, it was determined by the House that for the future all petitions or other papers touching slavery should be laid on the table without being debated, printed, read, or referred. For this resolution the friends of Mr. Van Buren unanimously voted.

Mr. Van Buren's third annual message, in December, 1839, was largely occupied with financial discussions, and especially with the argument for the divorce of the Government from the banks, and for the exclusive " receipt and payment of gold and silver in all public transactions " This measure, by which his administration is especially distinguished, became a law in 1840. The canvass preliminary to the Presidential election of 1840 was begun unusually early and with unwonted energy by the opposition. Mr. Van Buren was nominated for re-election at the Democratic National Convention held on the 5th of May, 1840. General Harrison was the Whig nominee. Never in the political history of the United States was a canvass conducted amid such absorbing public excitement, and never was a man more maligned or better abused than Martin Van Buren. The financial distress which had existed more or less oppressively during his administration was a standing text for the opposition journals and for the orators who assailed him at monster meetings in every part of the country. Charges of corruption, of extravagance, of indifference to the welfare of the laboring classes were brought against him in the most extravagant manner, while the enthusiasm of the supporters of General Harrison was inflamed by log cabins, emblematic of his popular origin and habits, by songs, by processions, by assemblages counting tens and hundreds of thousands.

In 1844 Mr. Van Buren's friends once more urged his nomination for the Presidency by the Democratic National Convention at Baltimore, but he was defeated then on account of his opposition to the annexation of Texas to the Union.

In 1848, when the Democrats had nominated Lewis Cass, and avowed their readiness to tolerate slavery in the new Territories lately acquired from Mexico, Mr. Van Buren and his adherents, adopting the name of the Free Democracy, at once began to discuss in public that new aspect of the slavery question. They held a convention at Utica on the 22d of June, which nominated Mr. Van Buren for President and Henry Dodge, of Wisconsin, for Vice-President. Mr. Dodge declined the nomination, and at a great convention held at Buffalo, on the 9th of August, Charles Francis Adams was substituted. The convention declared that " Congress had no more power to make a slave than to make a king." In accepting the nomination of this new party, Mr. Van Buren declared his full assent to its anti-slavery principles. In this contest Mr. Van Buren was defeated, and retired to private life on his estate at Kinderhook, where he died, July 24th, 1862. As a speaker, without any pretension to eloquence, Mr. Van Buren was logical and forcible, with a persuasiveness which even few of his gifted contemporaries could equal.

PRESIDENT MONROE'S FIRST CABINET.

Secretary of State.—John Quincy Adams, of Massachusetts, appointed March 5th, 1817.

Secretaries of the Treasury.—Albert Gallatin, of Pennsylvania, continued; William H. Crawford, of Georgia, appointed October 22d, 1817.

Secretaries of War.—William H. Crawford, of Georgia, continued; John C. Calhoun, of South Carolina, appointed December 15th, 1817.

Secretaries of the Navy.—Benjamin W. Crowninshield, of Massachusetts, continued; Smith Thompson, of New York, appointed November 9th, 1818.

Attorneys-General.—Richard Rush, of Pennsylvania, continued; William Wirt, of Virginia, appointed December 15th, 1817.

CHAPTER IX.

CAMPAIGN OF 1820.

REPUBLICAN NOMINEES.

For President.
JAMES MONROE of Virginia.

For Vice-President.
DANIEL D. TOMPKINS of New York.

FEDERAL NOMINEES FOR WHOM ELECTORAL VOTES WERE CAST.

For President.
JOHN QUINCY ADAMS of Massachusetts.

For Vice-President.
RICHARD STOCKTON of New Jersey.

CAUCUSES AND NOMINATIONS.

IN 1820 it was a foregone conclusion that Monroe and Tompkins were to be re-elected.

A call for a Republican nominating caucus was published early in April of that year, and in one week thereafter some fifty Republicans assembled in the House of Representatives; but owing to the limited attendance and the pronounced opposition to caucuses, the assembly disbanded.

The Federal party, at this time, was so dismembered, it presented no ticket.

Mr. Monroe received all the electoral votes but one, which was cast for John Quincy Adams.

Mr. Tompkins received all the electoral votes for Vice-President but fourteen. These were divided between Richard Stockton, Daniel Rodney, and Richard Rush.

Monroe's eight years of administration is known as the "Era of Good Feeling."

JOHN C. CALHOUN.

John C. Calhoun was born in Abbeville District, South Carolina, on the 18th of March, 1782. His father, Patrick Calhoun, was a native of Ireland, but emigrated with his parents to Pennsylvania in 1733. From thence the family removed to the west of Virginia; but being driven away by the Indians after the defeat of Braddock, they settled in South Carolina, on the borders of the Cherokee territory.

At the age of twenty young Calhoun was sent to Yale College, where he was graduated in 1804. He then entered the law school at Litchfield, Conn., and having completed his studies returned home, and was admitted to the bar in South Carolina. His great abilities as a public speaker immediately gave him prominence, and in 1808 he was chosen to the Legislature, in which he so distinguished himself that, in 1811, he was sent to Congress. From that period until his death he was an active participant in all the great events and questions which attracted public attention. After remaining six years in Congress he was appointed Secretary of War by President Monroe, and in 1825 was elected Vice-President of the United States.

In 1831 he was elected to a seat in the Senate, which position he held until 1843. The following year he was appointed Secretary of State by President Tyler, and in 1845 he was again returned to the Senate, of which body he continued a member till his death, which occurred at Washington on the 31st of March, 1850.

Shortly after the commencement of President's Monroe's second term, in 1821, the question of the successorship became one of leading interest. Calhoun's name was mentioned among others. He was regarded as a statesman of broad views, above mere local or narrow party influences. W. H. Crawford was also a candidate for the Presidency; but the military exploits of General Jackson made such an impression on the popular mind that the friends of Calhoun judged it expedient for them to withdraw his name and support Jackson instead. Thereupon Calhoun contented himself with running for the Vice-Presidency.

In 1844 Mr. Calhoun was again brought forward by his friends as a candidate for the Democratic nomination for the Presidency ; but instructions having been given to a majority of the delegates to the approaching nominating convention to vote for Mr. Van Buren, Calhoun, in February, addressed a letter to his political friends, severely criticising the principles on which the convention was to be constituted, and refusing to allow his name to be used.

As a public speaker Calhoun occupied the foremost rank among the great orators of any time or country. His diction was remarkable for the absence of ornament and metaphor, and for its clear, terse and logical compactness. Avoiding all discursiveness of the imagination, his speeches are characterized by a salient pressure to the point and a fiery vehemence of dogmatic argumentation unbroken in its flow. In earnestness he was never surpassed by even a religious devotee.

The following is in part Mr. Webster's estimate of him, delivered in the Senate when his death was announced : " The eloquence of Mr. Calhoun was a part of his intellectual character. It grew out of the qualities of his mind. It was plain, strong, wise, condensed, concise ; sometimes impassioned, still always severe. Rejecting ornament, not often seeking illustration, his power consisted in the plainness of his propositions, in the closeness of his logic, and in the earnestness and energy of his manner. No man was more respectful to others ; no man carried himself with greater decorum ; no man with superior dignity. I have not in public nor in private life known a more assiduous person in the discharge of his duty. His colloquial talents were singular and eminent. He had the basis—the indisputable basis—of all high character, unspotted integrity, and honor unimpeached. Firm in his purposes, patriotic and honest as I am sure he was in the principles he espoused and in the measures he defended, I do not believe that, aside from his large regard for that species of distinction that conducted him to eminent stations for the benefit of the Republic, he had a selfish motive or a selfish feeling."

PRESIDENT MONROE'S SECOND CABINET.

Secretary of State.—John Quincy Adams, of Massachusetts, continued.
Secretary of the Treasury.—William H. Crawford, of Georgia, continued.
Secretary of War.—John C. Calhoun, of South Carolina, continued.
Secretaries of the Navy.—Smith Thompson, of New York, continued; Samuel L. Southard, of New Jersey, appointed September 16th, 1823.
Attorney-General.—William Wirt, of Virginia, continued.

CHAPTER X.

CAMPAIGN OF 1824.

REPUBLICAN NOMINEES.

For President.

JOHN QUINCY ADAMS of Massachusetts.
GENERAL ANDREW JACKSON of North Carolina.
HENRY CLAY of Kentucky.
WILLIAM H. CRAWFORD of Georgia.

CONVENTIONS AND NOMINATIONS.

GENERAL JACKSON, Mr. Adams, and Mr. Clay were nominated by the Legislatures of their respective States, and these nominations were indorsed by the Legislatures of various other States according to preferences.

Mr. Crawford was a caucus candidate. That system of nomination was in such disrepute, the Republicans would not support any man nominated in that way.

The canvass which followed these nominations was exciting in the highest degree. The candidates were all Republicans. The issues were local and personal, and the contest of these great leaders bore the opprobrium of the "scrub race."

The election in November gave no candidate a majority of electors, and it devolved upon the House of Representatives to choose a President from the three highest on the list—Jackson, Adams, and Crawford. Clay, standing fourth on the list, was not eligible; but he gave his support to Adams, and the latter was elected by the votes of thirteen States. Seven States voted for Jackson and four for Crawford.

In the electoral college Jackson received 99 votes; Adams, 84; Crawford, 41; and Clay, 37. For Vice-President, John C. Calhoun received

182 electoral votes, and was elected to that office. Nathan Sanford received 30 electoral votes ; Nathaniel Macon, 24 ; Andrew Jackson, 13 ; Martin Van Buren, 9 ; and Henry Clay, 2.

The popular vote was as follows : Jackson, 155,872 ; Adams, 105,321 ; Crawford, 44,282 ; Clay, 46,587.

DANIEL WEBSTER.

Daniel Webster, the profound statesman and great orator, was born in the town of Salisbury, New Hampshire, on the 18th of January, 1782. In a speech delivered at Saratoga, in 1840, Mr. Webster said of his birthplace : " It did not happen to me to be born in a log cabin ; but my elder brothers and sisters were, which was raised amid the snow-drifts of New Hampshire at a period so early that, when the smoke first rose from its rude chimney and curled over the frozen hills, there was no similar evidence of a white man's habitation between it and the settlements on the rivers of Canada."

Amid the rugged, majestic scenery of the old Granite State Daniel Webster was reared, and there it was his youthful mind was impressed with scenes of grandeur and sublimity, which doubtless had a potent influence over the developments of his high moral and intellectual character, and so it was thought, years afterward, on a day memorable in Senatorial annals, when Mr. Webster pronounced " sentences of powerful thought, towering in accumulative grandeur, one above the other, as if he strove, Titan-like, to reach the very heavens themselves."

In 1796 young Webster was sent to Phillips Exeter Academy, and here the future statesman was first called upon to speak in public ; and it surely affords some encouragement to the diffident young student who is just commencing an oratorical career, to learn that Daniel Webster " evinced in his boyhood the strongest antipathy to public declamation—that in his first effort he became embarrassed, and even burst into tears."

Mr. Webster speaks of his earliest oratorical efforts at this school as follows : " I believe I made tolerable progress in most branches which I attended to ; but there was one thing I could not do. I could not make a declamation. I could not speak before the school. The kind and excellent Buckminster sought especially to persuade me to perform the exercise of declamation like other boys, but I could not do it. Many a piece did I commit to memory, and recite and rehearse in my own room, over and over again ; yet when the day came when the school collected to hear declamations, when my name was called and I saw all eyes turned to my seat, I could not raise myself from it. Sometimes the instructors frowned ; sometimes they smiled. Mr. Buckminster always pressed and entreated, most willingly, that I would venture. But I never could command sufficient resolution."

In 1797 he entered Dartmouth College, where he partly supported himself and aided his elder brother, Ezekiel, to prepare for college by teaching school in winter. He graduated in 1801, and immediately entered the law office of Thomas W. Thompson, his father's next-door neighbor, who was afterward a United States Senator. In 1804 Mr. Webster went to Boston and entered the office of Christopher Gore to complete his legal studies. In 1805 he was admitted to the bar, and commenced practice at Boscawen, New Hampshire. In 1806 he removed to Portsmouth, then the capital of the State. Here he made rapid progress, and was soon recognized as the leader at a bar composed of eminent counsel.

Mr. Webster came forward in life at a time when party spirit ran high. He had inherited from his father the principles of the Federal party, and advocated them in speeches and resolutions on public occasions, but did not for some years embark deeply in politics. The declaration of war in 1812, long foreseen and deprecated by the Federalists, created a demand or the best talent the country could furnish. Mr. Webster had already established a commanding reputation, and in 1812 he was elected a representative in Congress from the Portsmouth district as a Peace advocate, and in the organization of the House was placed on the Committee of Foreign Affairs. Early in the session he delivered his first speech to that body, and so great was its effect that he immediately took rank with the first debaters in Congress. He was re-elected in 1814.

In 1816 Mr. Webster removed to Boston. For nearly seven years after his removal, with a single exception, he filled no public office, but devoted himself exclusively to the practice of his profession, taking a position as a counsellor and an advocate above which no one has ever risen in this country.

In 1820 Mr. Webster was a member of the Massachusetts Convention to revise the Constitution of that State after the separation of Maine. During its session he pronounced, on December 22d, 1820, his celebrated discourse at Plymouth on the anniversary of the landing of the Pilgrim Fathers. This was the first of a series of performances, apart from the efforts of the Senate and the bar, by which he placed himself at the head of American orators. In the autumn of 1822 he was elected to Congress by a very large majority, and in 1824 was re-elected, receiving in seven wards of Boston 1986 votes, against one vote for Mr. Putnam. In 1827 he was elected to the Senate of the United States to fill a vacancy, and retained his seat by re-election till 1841.

In 1840 Mr. Webster was instrumental, more than any other leader, in bringing about the political change which was consummated in the election of General Harrison. During this spirited canvass Webster's voice was heard in the principal cities of the East in eloquent advocacy of the Harrison ticket. During this campaign, a good, pious acquaintance of Mr. Webster, who resided in New Hampshire, was suggested for State Senator. When he saw it announced that Mr. Webster was to speak in Faneuil Hall, he repaired to Boston to consult his distinguished friend and get his views on the propriety of his running for office. When he had acquainted the great statesman with the situation, Mr. Webster said : " I have too much respect for you to advise you to run for office. If you become a candidate the Democrats will say everything bad about you and try to defame your character. Why, they might even accuse you of stealing horses." This was hardly the advice which the man, whose vanity had been flattered by the mention of his name in connection with a State Senatorship, hoped to receive, yet he recognized its soundness ; but his secret ambition and the entreaties of other friends overcame his judgment, and he entered into the contest. Meeting Mr. Webster in Boston after the election, the Massachusetts statesman asked his New Hampshire friend how the election went with him. " Well, Mr. Webster," he said, " you know you told me if I ran for office the Democrats would say everything bad about me. They did ; and, as you predicted, they even accused me of stealing horses, and they almost proved it, too, and that's what beat me."

General Harrison, as soon as it was ascertained that he was elected, offered to Mr. Webster the choice of places in his cabinet. In 1844 he supported Mr. Clay's nomination for the Presidency, and in 1845 was again elected to the Senate, taking his seat as the successor of Rufus Choate. In 1848 Mr. Webster's friends had calculated, with some confidence, that the Whig nomination for President would fall upon him ; but General Taylor was made the nominee, and Mr. Webster advocated his election in speeches all through the Eastern and Middle States. In 1850 Mr. Webster resigned his seat in the Senate, having been appointed Secretary of State by President Fillmore, which office he held until his death, at Marshfield, on the 24th of October, 1852. In the spring of 1852 Mr. Webster's friends entertained sanguine hopes that he would receive the Whig nomination for President; but the choice of the convention held at Baltimore fell to General Scott.

The great speech of Mr. Webster, in reply to Colonel Hayne, is regarded as the ablest of his productions, and may be pronounced, said Mr. Everett, the most celebrated speech ever delivered in Congress. In many respects it was the greatest oratorical effort ever made by any statesman in ancient or modern times. In that marvellous speech Mr. Webster repelled the attacks of Colonel Hayne on the *Old Bay* State as follows : " Mr. President, I shall enter on no encomium upon Massachusetts. There she is— behold her, and judge for yourselves. There is her history ; the world knows it by heart. The past, at least, is secure. There is Boston, and Concord, and Lexington, and Bunker Hill—and there they will remain forever. The bones of her sons, falling in the great struggle for independence, now lie mingled with the soil of every State, from New England to Georgia ; and there they will lie forever. And, sir, where American Liberty raised its first voice, and where its youth was nurtured and sustained, there it still lives, in the strength of its manhood and full of its original spirit. If discord and disunion shall wound it—if party strife and blind ambition shall hawk and tear it—if folly and madness—if uneasiness, under salutary and necessary restraint, shall succeed to separate it from that Union, by which alone its existence is made sure, it will stand, in the end, by the side of that cradle in which its infancy was rocked ; it will stretch forth its arm, with whatever of vigor it may still retain, over the friends who gather around it, and it will fall at last, if fall it must, amid the proudest monuments of its own glory and on the very spot of its origin."

At the grand ceremonial of the laying of the corner-stone of the addition to the Capitol, on the 4th of July, 1851, Mr. Webster delivered the last of his most eloquent addresses. It was one of the noblest of his oratorical efforts—a magnificent burst of the highest eloquence.

THOMAS EWING.

Thomas Ewing was born in Ohio County, Virginia, December 28th, 1789, and died at Lancaster, Ohio, October 26th, 1871. The poverty of his early life and his successful overcomings of environments is but an additional unit in the large column of Amercian individual successes.

In his twentieth year he left home and worked in the Kanawha salt establishments until he had laid up money enough to pay for the farm which his father had purchased in 1792, in what is now Athens County, Ohio, and enabled himself to enter the Ohio University at Athens, where he graduated in 1815.

He studied law in Lancaster, Ohio, was admitted to the bar in 1816, and practised with great success in the State courts and the Supreme Court of the United States.

In March, 1831, he took his seat in the United States Senate. He spoke against confirming the nomination of Van Buren as Minister to Great Britain, supported the protective tariff system of Clay, and advocated a reduction of the rates of postage, a recharter of the United States Bank, and the Revenue Collection bill, known as the "Force bill." In 1834 and again in 1835, as a member of the Committee on Post-Offices and Post Roads, he presented a majority report on abuses in the post-office, which resulted in the reorganization of that department. He opposed the removal of the deposits from the United States Bank, and on December 21st, 1835, introduced a bill for the settlement of the Ohio boundary question, which was passed March 11th and June 15th, 1836. During the same session he brought forward a bill, which became a law, for the reorganization of the general land office ; and on several occasions he opposed the policy of granting pre-emption rights to settlers on the public lands. He spoke against the admission of Michigan, and presented a memorial for the abolition of slavery and the slave trade in the District of Columbia, which, he insisted, ought to be referred, though he was opposed to granting the prayer of the memorialists.

In July, 1836, the Secretary of the Treasury issued what was known as the "specie circular," directing receivers in land offices to accept payments only in gold, silver, or treasury certificates, except from certain classes of persons, for a limited time.

GEORGE WILLIAM CURTIS.

In December Mr. Ewing brought in a bill to annul this circular, and another declaring it unlawful for the secretary to make such discrimination ; but the bills were not carried.

His term expired in March, 1837, and he resumed the practice of his profession.

In 1841 he was appointed Secretary of the Treasury by President Harrison, and retained that office under President Tyler. His first official report proposed the imposition of twenty per cent *ad valorem* duties on certain articles for the relief of the national debt, disapproved the independent Treasury Act, passed the preceding year, and urged the establishment of a national bank. He was requested to prepare a bill for the last purpose, which was passed with some alteration, but was vetoed by the President. Mr. Tyler thereupon indicated a plan for a bank of moderate capital for the regulation of exchanges, and at his request Mr. Ewing helped to frame a charter, which was immediately passed, and, in turn, vetoed. Mr. Ewing, with all the other members of the cabinet except Mr. Webster, consequently resigned in September, 1841.

On the accession of General Taylor to the Presidency, in 1849, he took office as Secretary of the newly-created Department of the Interior, which he organized. Among the measures recommended in his first report, December 3d, 1849, were the extension of the public land laws to California, New Mexico, and Oregon, the establishment of a mint near the California gold mines, and the construction of a road to the Pacific.

On the death of Taylor and the accession of Fillmore, in 1850, Mr. Corwin became Secretary of the Treasury, and Mr. Ewing was appointed by the Governor of Ohio to serve during Corwin's unexpired term in the Senate. In this body he refused to vote for the Fugitive Slave bill, opposed Clay's Compromise bill, reported on the Committee from Finance a bill for the establishment of a branch mint in California, and advocated a reduction of postage, river and harbor appropriations, and the abolition of slavery in the District of Columbia.

In 1851 he retired from public life, and resumed the practice of law at Lancaster.

Among the most elaborate of his written professional arguments are those in the cases of Oliver *v.* Piatt, *et al*, involving the title to a large part of Toledo, Ohio ; the Methodist Church division ; the McIntire poor school *v.* Zanesville ; and the McMicken will, involving large bequests for education.

He was delegate to the Peace Congress of 1860, and was also chosen a delegate to the National Union Convention in 1866.

During the war he gave the Union cause an unflinching support.

His son-in-law, General William T. Sherman, and his son, General Thomas Ewing, Jr., were, as is well known, among the most conspicuous of the Union generals.

During his last years, in consequence of infirmities, he lived in complete retirement, yet he preserved to the end a keen interest in the nation's wonderful growth and prosperity.

PRESIDENT ADAMS'S CABINET.

Secretary of State. —Henry Clay, of Kentucky, appointed March 7th, 1825.

Secretary of the Treasury. —Richard Rush, of Pennsylvania, appointed March 7th, 1825

Secretaries of War. —James Barbour, of Virginia, appointed March 7th, 1825 ; Peter B. Potter, of New York, appointed May 26th, 1828.

Secretary of the Navy. —Samuel L. Southard, of New Jersey, continued.

Attorney-General. —William Wirt, of Virginia, continued.

CHAPTER XI.

CAMPAIGN OF 1828.

DEMOCRATIC NOMINEES.

For President.
ANDREW JACKSON of Tennessee.

For Vice-President.
JOHN C. CALHOUN of South Carolina.

NATIONAL REPUBLICAN NOMINEES.

For President.
JOHN QUINCY ADAMS of Massachusetts.

For Vice-President.
RICHARD RUSH of Pennsylvania.

CAUCUSES, CONVENTIONS, AND NOMINATIONS.

EARLY in the administration of John Quincy Adams a fierce canvass was carried on in the House of Representatives for the succeeding term. The Legislature of Tennessee seconded the choice of the friends of General Jackson in the House, and nominated him in October, 1825. The Assembly of Massachusetts followed the action of the Tennessee Legislature, and nominated Mr. Adams for a second term.

Numerous conventions in the several States followed, and both candidates were favored. This was at a period when the caucus system was in disfavor, and national conventions had not yet come in vogue.

The electoral count gave Jackson one hundred and seventy-eight votes, and John Quincy Adams eighty-three.

WILLIAM WIRT.

William Wirt was born at Bladensburg, near Washington, on the 8th of November, 1782. His father died when he was an infant, and his mother when he was but eight years old. Like many great men, he was early left orphaned of everything but resolution and hope, to battle with worldly adversity, and, in the midst of struggles, to build his fortunes.

After suitable preparatory studies he went to Leesburg, Virginia, and when seventeen years old commenced the study of law, and three years later was admitted to the bar.

Young Wirt rose rapidly in his profession, and so eminent had he become, that he was retained in the Aaron Burr prosecution in 1807, and to him, as much as to any of the counsel engaged, belonged the commendation of the court that " a degree of eloquence, seldom displayed on any occasion, embellished solidity of argument, and depth of research."

In 1816 Mr. Madison appointed Mr. Wirt Attorney for Virginia ; and in the following year he was appointed Attorney-General of the United States by President Monroe. This office he held continuously for eleven years and four months.

In 1826, at the request of the citizens of Washington, he delivered an eulogy on Adams and Jefferson. It was regarded one of the most masterly productions which that melancholy event occasioned.

Those who were familiar with the clearness, melody, and flexibility of Wirt's voice when at the height of his fame, and his distinct, emphatic, and pure pronunciation, were surprised to learn that when he entered on the practice of his profession " his utterance was thick—his tongue clumsy and apparently too large—his pronunciation of words clipping, and when excited by feeling his voice unmanageable, sometimes bursting out in loud, harsh, indistinct, and imperfect articulation." All this he overcame through persevering and resistless cultivation. All through his life he was a passionate and persevering votary of elocution. But over and above the mere verbiage of his spoken thought, he gave great attention to gesture, which is " the language of the body." " The hands are the common language of mankind," said Cicero, and another distinguished Roman orator was accustomed to declare that " he was never fit to talk till he had ' warmed his arm.' " There can be no doubt that Wirt's genius was of the highest order, but he began and continued through his whole splendid career under the deep conviction that eminent success depended on the most assiduous self-cultivation, and his diligent and unremitting discipline may claim a share of credit for the brilliant success which he achieved in the field of oratory. In 1832 Mr. Wirt was the nominee of the anti-Mason party for the Presidency. 'He developed the full strength of the party, and received seven electoral votes. He died in the city of Washington on the 18th of February, 1834.

PRESIDENT JACKSON'S FIRST CABINET.

Secretaries of State.—Martin Van Buren, of New York, appointed March 6th, 1829; Edward Livingston, of Louisiana, appointed May 24th, 1831.

Secretaries of the Treasury.—Samuel D. Ingham, of Pennsylvania, appointed March 6th, 1829; Louis McLane, of Delaware, appointed August 8th, 1831.

Secretaries of War.—John H. Eaton, of Tennessee, appointed March 9th, 1829; Lewis Cass, of Michigan, appointed August 1st, 1831.

Secretaries of the Navy.—John Branch, of North Carolina, appointed March 9th, 1829; Levi Woodbury, of New Hampshire, appointed May 23d, 1831.

Postmaster-General.—William B. Barry, of Kentucky, appointed March 9th, 1829.

Attorneys-General.—John M. Berrien, of Georgia, appointed March 9th, 1829; Roger B. Taney, of Maryland, appointed December 27th, 1831.

CHAPTER XII.

CAMPAIGN OF 1832.

DEMOCRATIC NOMINEES.

For President.
ANDREW JACKSON of Tennessee.

For Vice-President.
MARTIN VAN BUREN of New York.

NATIONAL REPUBLICAN NOMINEES.

For President.
HENRY CLAY of Kentucky.

For Vice-President.
JOHN SERGEANT of Pennsylvania.

CONVENTIONS AND NOMINATIONS.

THE first national political convention held in the United States was that convened at Philadelphia in September, 1830, by the anti-Masonic party, an organization which grew out of the excitement incident to the mysterious disappearance of Morgan, a royal arch Mason, in September, 1826.

The convention passed a resolution to adjourn to the 26th day of September, 1831, at Baltimore, and make suitable nominations for the offices of President and Vice-President. The Baltimore Convention, which assembled in pursuance of the foregoing resolution, nominated William Wirt, of Maryland, and Amos Ellmaker, of Pennsylvania,

The National Republicans held a convention at Baltimore on the 12th of December, 1831, and nominated Henry Clay for President and John Sergeant for Vice-President, by a unanimous vote.

The Democratic party, in the same city, at its first national convention, presented as its choice General Jackson for President and Martin Van Buren for Vice-President.

EDWARD EVERETT.

Edward Everett was born in Dorchester, near Boston, April 11th, 1794. At the age of ten his regular preparation for college was begun, and he was sent to a private school kept by Ezekiel Webster, of New Hampshire; a gentleman, says Mr. Everett himself, "of eminent talent and great worth, well entitled to be remembered for his own sake, but better known as the elder brother of Daniel Webster." On one occasion, during the absence of his brother, Daniel Webster took charge of the school for a week. It was thus that an acquaintance began which afterward ripened into the closest regard. Few things, probably, were less in the thought of either, in that schoolhouse, than that the boy, as Governor of Massachusetts, would one day sign the commission of his teacher as Senator of the United States, or, at a later day, succeed him in the State Department.

Young Everett entered Harvard College in the summer of 1807, and graduating four years later, entered immediately on the study of divinity. In 1813 he was invited and accepted the call to become the pastor of the Brattle Square Church, in Boston. In 1815 he was called by the government of Harvard College to the chair of the Greek professorship. Accepting their invitation, he made his first visit to Europe to prepare for his new duties. Returning to America in 1819, after a long course of study and travel, he entered upon the professorship, which he held until his election to Congress, from the Middlesex District, in 1824.

He took his seat in the House of Representatives in 1825 as a supporter of Mr. Adams, and served there for ten years. He was at once appointed to the Committee on Foreign Affairs. To the foreign relations of the country, therefore, he gave especial attention; but his interest was not limited to them. These years were marked by discussions on the most important interests in our legislation, and in many of these discussions he took a leading place.

In 1835 Mr. Everett was elected Governor of Massachusetts, and held that office for the four years following. In 1839 he failed of a re-election by a single vote, and in 1840 sailed for Europe and passed the winter in Italy. General Harrison's election, however, brought his political friends into favor, and Mr. Everett was appointed Minister at the Court of St. James. The questions relating to the North-eastern boundary, the fisheries, the Caroline, the Creole, the case of McLeod, and other matters of dispute were then at their most critical stage.

Mr. Webster's intimate knowledge of the powers and qualifications of his friend gave the latter full scope for unfettered action; and never, it is safe to say, was a difficult diplomatic duty discharged with more judgment, delicacy, and grace. Returning home in 1846, Mr. Everett was recalled to academic life by his Alma Mater, which in that year elected him president, to succeed the venerable Josiah Quincy. Holding this position for three years, he resigned it in 1849, and for some years remained in comparative retirement. At the death of Mr. Webster, in October, 1852, Mr. Everett was called by President Fillmore to the Department of State. During the few months that he was Secretary of State he had occasion, in the matter of the proposed tripartite convention respecting Cuba, to leave upon record a memorable token of the reach and vigor of his policy in foreign affairs.

The change of administration, however, withdrew him from office, and in 1853 he took his seat in the United States Senate. His health, under the pressure of official toil, failed him, and in May, 1854, he resigned his seat; and this event terminated his career in public office in the service of the nation, with a single memorable exception.

The great work which he performed in the next four years, when, with infirm bodily powers, he labored incessantly for the Mount Vernon Fund, will command admiration as long as his name shall be remembered.

The sum collected by his efforts for this noble object was nearly one hundred thousand dollars; but the motives which actuated him to this great work were still more beneficent. He believed that a contemplation of the character and spirit of the immortal founder of the Republic would serve to allay the excitement and bitterness of feeling which the slavery question had produced between the Northern and Southern States. In a public speech he alluded to his efforts in behalf of the Mount Vernon cause as follows:

"After the sectional warfare of opinion and feeling reached a dangerous height, anxious, if possible, to bring a counteractive and conciliating influence into play—feeling that there was yet one golden chord of sympathy which ran throughout the land—in the hope of contributing something, however small, to preserve what remained, and restore what was lost of kind feeling between the two sections of the country, I devoted the greater part of my time for three years to the attempt to give new strength in the hearts of my countrymen to the last patriotic feeling in which they seemed to beat in entire unison—veneration and love for the name of Washington, and reverence for the place of his rest. With this object in view, I travelled thousands of miles, by night and by day, in midwinter and midsummer, speaking three, four, and five times a week, in feeble health, and under a heavy burden of domestic care and sorrow, and including the priceless value of the Union in precisely the same terms from Maine to Georgia and from New York to St. Louis."

In 1860 Mr. Everett was nominated for the Vice-Presidency by the American or Compromise party, with the Hon. John Bell, of Tennessee, as the candidate for the Presidency. But the time for compromises was past, and both North and South eagerly nerved themselves for the approaching conflict. The American party received only one eighth of the electoral vote.

Perceiving that war was inevitable, and satisfied that he had done all that was in his power to avert it, he accepted the issue, and henceforth devoted all his energies to the support of the Federal Government. The single exception alluded to, in which Mr. Everett once more discharged a high public function in the national service, was his fulfilment of the imposing charge given him by the people of Massachusetts, when they chose him their Presidential elector, in November, 1864. The last occasion on which his voice was heard in public was at a meeting held in Faneuil Hall on Monday, January 12th, 1865, for the relief of the people of Savannah. He died three days later, in the seventy-first year of his age.

To Everett, as an orator, must be accorded the finest and most complete proportions that have marked any speaker of the century. The mould of personal form, all the graces, the voice, the cadences, partly constitutional and partly acquired, all that is histrionic and attractive, all that nature could furnish and art could add, belonged in largest measure and in purest style to him.

RUFUS CHOATE.

Rufus Choate is to be ranked as the greatest American advocate. He was an able lawyer, a shining statesman, an all-accomplished man of letters. He will be remembered always as holding the same relation to America that Curran held to Ireland and Erskine to Great Britain.

Rufus Choate was born in Ipswich, Massachusetts, October 1st, 1799, and died in July, 1859, in the sixtieth year of his age.

He is known to the world outside of his profession of the law chiefly by his speeches in the United States Senate and his addresses to the people on political and literary subjects from the caucus and lyceum platforms. He grew up in Essex County, Massachusetts, with but ordinary opportunities of schooling. When he was sixteen years old he entered Dartmouth College, but a brilliant boyhood had already made him sufficiently known to excite in many quarters of old Essex strong hopes of his future. His college course increased these expectations. After graduating he taught school, but soon adopted the law as his profession. He entered the Dane Law School, remaining there a few months, and then, leaving his Essex home, continued his studies in Washington, in the office of William Wirt, then Attorney-General of the United States. He stayed in this office one year. He had the good fortune to hear the last great argument of William Pickney and one of the first of Daniel Webster in the Senate. He then entered the office of Judge Cummins, of Salem, and in September, 1823, he was admitted to the bar of Common Pleas of that county, and opened an office in the town of Danvers, near by. In two or three years he removed to Salem, and in 1825 was admitted to the bar of the Supreme Judicial Court. His success was almost instantaneous.

In 1825 he was elected to the Legislature of Massachusetts, and in 1827 was a member of the State Senate. In 1832 he was elected to Congress from the Essex district, but declined a re-election. In these occasional forays into politics he distinguished himself by set speeches, florid, erudite, and fervid.

A friend of Mr. Choate, referring to his election to Congress, said: "We all rejoiced in his honors, he bore them so meekly. He never sought office; office always sought him."

In 1841 he took Mr. Webster's chair in the Senate when that gentleman entered General Harrison's Cabinet.

In the Senate he made those speeches which have most drawn upon him the attention of a nation. Most of them were carefully revised by himself and officially published. The speech on the Oregon question, in reply to Mr. Buchanan, those on the tariff, the annexation of Texas, to provide further remedial justice in the courts of the United States, were of leading importance.

In the Senate he was regarded as the especial friend and expounder of the views of the Secretary of State, Mr. Webster. This led to an unfortunate encounter between him and Mr. Clay, who was enraged at Webster's remaining in office under President Tyler.

His style of Senatorial address was the same passionate and pictorial stream of speech as his jury appeals. The Southern and Western men, especially, spoke with enthusiasm of that dark-faced Senator from Massachusetts, with curling locks and such a delightful flow of words.

In 1845 he returned to the practice of the profession of which he was so fond, and in which he was working when death found him, still busy.

When he left the Senate his public life may be said to have closed. From then on the strictly professional current of his life was only broken by his hurried visit to Europe, in 1850, his addresses, and his services in the Constitutional Convention of Massachusetts.

Of his political addresses, the ones in which he seemed to throw his heart most warmly and his imagination most brilliantly, were those of the campaign of 1848, which closed with the election of General Taylor to the Presidency, and those of the campaign of the compromises, which ended with the defeat of Daniel Webster for the nomination to that office.

In the career of the frontier captain, Zachary Taylor; his intrepid march of victory from Monterey to Buena Vista; his answer to Santa Anna when summoned to surrender, the vivid imagination of Mr. Choate found fitting field.

His love of Webster was at once womanly and Homeric. In his speech of March, 1852, he closed a highly-wrought peroration by a singularly homely and practical illustration, which exemplified the startling anti-climax, always one of his oratoric weapons. When in summing up the thoughts which for an hour he had hurled upon the crowded audience surging in the vast hall before him, he reached what appeared to be the acme of powerful eulogium upon Webster; he suddenly stopped, threw himself forward in the attitude in which a sailor would heave on rope on the ship's deck. "Now, boys," he exclaimed, "don't you think he'd be a good pilot?" There was a great response from the crowd. "Then, altogether now, and heave him on to the quarter-deck."

The public address to which he devoted the most study of his life was his oration on Mr. Webster, delivered at Dartmouth College in August, 1853.

A description of Mr. Choate during his prime was penned by a friend. "Mr. Choate was rather a tall and full-sized man, and looked worn, but sturdy and muscular. He was strongly built, with big bones, broad shoulders, large feet and bony hands, and of a tough fibre in his general physique. More than this, he had the nervous, bilious temperament—the temperament for hard work, as well as brilliant work. His chest was wide and powerful, and his floating hair, which is, in some degree, a test of a strong constitution, resisted all the inflammation of his busy brain, and remained to the last firmly set. It was always black, and hardly tinged with those gray hues which have been called the 'white flag of truce which old age hangs out to the hatreds of life.' He was a very strong man, capable of vast fatigue. From his frequent sick-headaches and the appearance of his face, many supposed him a feeble man. It was not feebleness, but immense overwork which eventually wore him down."

PRESIDENT JACKSON'S SECOND CABINET.

Secretaries of State.—Edward Livingston, of Louisiana, continued; Louis McLane, of Delaware, appointed May 29th, 1833; John Forsyth, of Georgia, appointed June 27th, 1834.

Secretaries of the Treasury.—Louis McLane, of Delaware, continued; William I. Duane, of Pennsylvania, appointed May 29th, 1833; Levi Woodbury, of New Hampshire, appointed June 27th, 1834.

Secretary of War.—Lewis Cass, of Michigan, continued.

Secretaries of the Navy.—Levi Woodbury, of New Hampshire, continued; Mahlon Dickerson, of New Jersey, appointed June 30th, 1834.

Postmasters-General.—William T. Barry, of Kentucky, continued; Amos Kendall, of Kentucky, appointed May 1st, 1835.

Attorneys-General.—Roger B. Taney, of Maryland, continued; Benjamin F. Butler, of New York, appointed June 24th, 1834.

HORATIO SEYMOUR.

CHAPTER XIII.

CAMPAIGN OF 1836.

DEMOCRATIC NOMINEES.

For President.
MARTIN VAN BUREN of NewYork.

For Vice-President.
RICHARD M. JOHNSON of Kentucky.

WHIG NOMINEES.

For President.
WILLIAM HENRY HARRISON of Ohio.

For Vice-President.
FRANCIS GRANGER of New York.

CONVENTIONS AND NOMINATIONS.

THE Democratic party, in a national convention held at Baltimore on the 16th day of May, 1835, nominated Martin Van Buren for President and Richard M. Johnson for Vice-President.

The Whigs held a convention at Albany on the 3d day of February, 1836, and nominated General William H. Harrison for President and Francis Granger for Vice-President. Delegates were only present from New York State.

The anti-Masons, at their second national convention, indorsed the Albany nominations.

Hugh L. White, of Tennessee, Daniel Webster, of Massachusetts, and Willie P. Mingum, of North Carolina, were candidates before the people.

The election gave Van Buren 170 electoral votes; General Harrison, 73; Hugh L. White, 26; Webster, 14, and Mingum, 11.

WENDELL PHILLIPS.

Wendell Phillips, the great Abolition orator, was born in Boston, Massachusetts, on the 29th of November, 1811, and died in his native city on the 2d of February, 1884.

A thorough preparatory course of study preceded his admission to Harvard College in 1827, from which institution he graduated in 1831. Three years later he was admitted to the bar, and shortly thereafter he was a witness of the mob in which Garrison was dragged disgracefully through the streets of Boston for the crime of speaking his conscientious opinions. This scene made a deep impression on young Phillips, and a resolution was then formed in his mind to do what he could for the cause of liberty. The shooting of Rev. E. P. Lovejoy at Albion, Illinois, on the 7th of December, 1837, by a mob, while attempting to defend his printing-press from destruction, was another event which moved his feelings and gave him his first subject for his first public speech. When the news of this event was received in Boston, Dr. Channing headed a petition to the mayor and aldermen asking the use of Faneuil Hall, in which to hold a public meeting to express indignation at the outrage.

It will hardly be credited by the present generation that a request so reasonable and so natural should have been denied. The mayor and aldermen of Boston in those days would do naught to offend Southern masters, and however well disposed toward their own distinguished citizens, dared not encourage them in the expression of any sentiments which might possibly be disagreeable to the South. This was the third printing-press which Lovejoy had attempted to defend. Dr. Channing, undismayed by the first rebuff, addressed an impressive letter to his fellow-citizens, which resulted in a meeting of influential gentlemen at the old court-room. Here measures were taken to secure a much larger number of names to the petition, and this being accomplished, the mayor and aldermen consented to the use of the historic hall. The meeting was held on the 8th of December, with the Hon. Jonathan Phillips as chairman. Dr. Channing opened the meeting with an eloquent address, and resolutions prepared by him were read and offered.

The Attorney-General of Massachusetts appeared now as the advocate of the assailants of Lovejoy. He compared the slaves, for whose liberty the sympathetic editor had pleaded, to a menagerie of wild beasts, and the Alton rioters to the orderly mob who threw the tea overboard in Boston Harbor in 1773 ; talked of the " conflict of laws" between Missouri and Illinois ; declared that Lovejoy was presumptuous and imprudent, and died as the fool or idiot. Then, with direct and insulting reference to Dr. Channing, he asserted that a clergyman with a gun in his hand, or one mingling in the debates of a popular assembly, were equally out of place.

This speech produced much sensation in the hall, and Wendell Phillips, who had come only as an interested spectator, without expecting to speak, rose immediately to his feet, and amid the boisterous confusion, which was started to drown his voice, proceeded to address the assemblage. That solemn and impressive demeanor which was his, was present with him then. That immense force which he always seemed to hold in reserve, and which, if he were to let out, would annihilate any object of his attack, was shown on that occasion. " Sir," he said, in the course of this speech, " when I heard the gentleman lay down principles which place the murderers of Alton side by side with Otis and Hancock, with Quincy and Adams, I thought those precious lips (pointing to the portraits in the hall) would have broken into voices to rebuke the recreant American ; the slander of the dead. . . . Sir, for the sentiments that he has uttered, on soil consecrated by the prayers of the Puritans and the blood of patriots, the earth should have yawned and swallowed him up." A storm of mingled applause and hisses interrupted the bold young orator, with cries of " Take that back— take that back !" The confusion for a time was so great he could not be heard.

Mr. Phillips came forward to the edge of the platform, and looking on the excited throng with that calm, firm, severe look which never failed to subdue an excited assemblage, said, solemnly : " Fellow-citizens, I cannot take back my words. Surely the attorney-general, so long and well known here, needs not the aid of your hisses against one so young as I am--my voice never before heard in your walls." After this the young orator received the respectful attention of the audience without interruption. In further allusion to the speech of the attorney-general, he said : "*Impudent* to defend the liberty of the press ! Why ? Because the defence was unsuccessful ! Does success gild crime into patriotism and the want of it change heroic self-devotion into imprudence ? Was Hampden imprudent when he drew the sword and threw away the scabbard ? Yet he, judged by that single hour, was unsuccessful. After a short exile the race he hated sat again upon the throne.

"Imagine yourselves present when the first news of Bunker Hill battle reached a New England town. The tale would have run thus : 'The patriots are routed—the red-coats victorious—Warren lies dead upon the field.' With what scorn would that Tory have been received who should have charged Warren with imprudence, who should have said that, 'bred a physician, he was out of place, and died as the fool dieth.' How would the intimation have been received that Warren and his successors should have waited a better time ?

"*Presumptuous* to assert the freedom of the press on American ground ! Is the assertion of such freedom before the age ? So much before the age as to leave no one a right to make it because it displeases the community ? Who invented this libel on his country ? It is this very thing which entitled Lovejoy to greater praise. The disputed right which provoked the revolution was far beneath that for which he died. As much as thought is better than money, so much is the cause in which Lovejoy died nobler than a mere question of taxes. James Otis thundered in this hall when the king did but touch his *pocket.* Imagine, if you can, his indignant eloquence if England had offered to put a gag on his lips. Mr. Chairman, from the bottom of my heart I thank that brave little band at Alton for resisting." Wendell Phillips arose the morning after his first speech to find himself famous as a great orator for the cause of liberty, as Patrick Henry had awakened to a similar realization nearly seventy-five years before.

From that time Wendell Phillips was identified with the radical Abolitionists. His nature led him at once to take the most strenuous and vigorous grounds side by side with William Lloyd Garrison. He believed the Constitution of the United States, by an incidental complicity with slavery, had become a sinful compact—'a covenant with death and an agreement with hell'—and with the unquestioning consistency which belonged to his Puritan blood, he did not hesitate to sacrifice to this belief his whole professional future. He abandoned his legal practice, and took leave of the Suffolk bar, because he could not conscientiously take the oath to support the Constitution of the United States.

Mrs. Stowe says, in her biography: "Henceforth there was no career open to him but that of the agitator and popular reformer. He brought to the despised and unfashionable cause not only the prestige of one of the most honored Massachusetts names, and the traditions of a family which was among orthodox circles as a Hebrew of the Hebrews, but the power of decidedly the first forensic orator that America has ever produced. His style was so dazzling, so brilliant, his oratory so captivating, that even the unpopularity of his sentiments could not prevent the multitudes from flocking to hear him. He had in a peculiar degree that mesmeric power of control which distinguishes the true orator, by which he holds a multitude subject to his will, and carries them whither he pleases.

"His speeches were generally extempore, and flowed on with a wonderful correctness and perfect finish of language, without faltering, without the shadow of an inelegance, his sentences succeeding one another with a poised and rhythmical fulness, and his illustrations happily running through the field of ancient and modern history, and with the greatest ease selecting whatever he needed from thence for the illustration of his subject. In invective no American or English orator has ever surpassed him. At the bar of his fervid oratory he would arraign, try, and condemn with a solemn and dignified earnestness that might almost have persuaded the object of his attack of his own guilt."

Mr. Phillips had a way of making his fame and reputation gain him a hearing on the unpopular subject which he had most at heart. Committees from anxious lyceums used to wait on him for his terms, sure of being able to fill a house by his name.

"What are your terms, Mr. Phillips?"

"If I lecture on anti-slavery, nothing. If on any other subject, one hundred dollars."

When the war was ended and the emancipation of the slave became a realization of Mr. Phillips's hope and labor, the great work of his life was finished, as the class of gifts and faculties which he possessed, and which are essential to force attention to neglected truths, were not those most adapted to the delicate work of reconstruction. "The good knight who can cut and hew in battle cannot always do the surgeon's work of healing and restoring. That exacting ideality which is the leading faculty of Mr. Phillips's nature leads him constantly to undervalue what has been attained, and it is to be regretted that it deprived him of the glow and triumph of a victory in which no man than he better deserved to rejoice.

"Garrison hung up his shield and sword at a definite point, and marked the era of victory with devout thankfulness ; and we can but regret that the more exacting mind of Phillips was too much fixed on what yet was wanting to share the well-earned joy.

"When there is strong light there must be shadow, and the only shadow we discern in the public virtues of Mr. Phillips is the want of a certain power to appreciate and make allowances for the necessary weaknesses and imperfections of human nature."

CALEB CUSHING.

The seemingly antagonistic callings of lawyer, soldier, and statesman were happily blended in Caleb Cushing, who was born at Salisbury, Massachusetts, January 17th, 1800.

Mr. Cushing was a member of a family that has been noted in Massachusetts from the early colonial days.

He graduated at Harvard College in 1818, and afterward became a student at the college for two years in moral philosophy, mathematics, and law. After continuing the study of law for five years he was admitted to practice, and settled in Newburyport. While he rose rapidly in the legal profession, he did not neglect literature or abstain from political pursuits. He was a frequent contributor to the *North American Review* and other periodicals.

He was, in 1825, chosen a member of the Lower House of the State Legislature, and one year later was elected a Senator. In 1829 he visited Europe on a tour of pleasure, and remained abroad nearly two years. On his return to Massachusetts he published an "Historical and Political Review" of European affairs, consequent on the occurrences of the French Revolution of 1830, and also his "Reminiscences of Spain."

He was again sent to the Legislature for the years 1833 and 1834, and finally represented the Essex district in the Lower House of Congress. To this position he was three times re-elected, serving regularly until March, 1843. He supported John Quincy Adams for the Presidency, and was a Whig until the accession of Mr. Tyler, whose administration he supported, and became classed as a Democrat. In 1843 President Tyler nominated him as Secretary of the Treasury, but the nomination was rejected by the

Senate. In the summer of that year he went to China as commissioner, and in 1844 negotiated the first treaty of the United States Government with China. On his return he was again elected a Representative in the Massachusetts Legislature, and in 1847 he raised a regiment for the Mexican War, furnishing the requisite money to equip the same. He was then appointed colonel of the regiment, and in the spring of 1847 accompanied it to Mexico. He was attached to the army of General Taylor, and soon after received the appointment of brigadier-general. While still in Mexico, in 1847 and 1848, he was nominated by the Democratic party of Massachusetts, but was defeated. In 1850, for the sixth time, he represented Newburyport in the Legislature. In the same year he was selected as the first mayor of that city, and was re-elected the following year. In 1852 he was appointed a justice of the Massachusetts Supreme Court, a post which he filled until March, 1853, when he was appointed by President Pierce United States Attorney-General, from which office he retired March 4th, 1857. Again he became a member of the Massachusetts Legislature, and co-operated with the Democratic party in its opposition to the anti-slavery aggressions. In April, 1861, he tendered his services to Governor Andrew, "in any capacity, however humble, in which it may be possible for me to contribute to the public weal in the present critical emergency." The governor, an ardent anti slavery and war champion, did not respond.

His services were often employed during the war in the departments at Washington, and in 1866 he was appointed commissioner to codify the laws of Congress. In 1868 he was sent to Bogota to arrange a diplomatic difficulty.

President Grant appointed him one of the American counsel before the tribunal of arbitration that was provided for by the treaty of Washington for the settlement of the Alabama claims, which met at Geneva in 1871, and concluded its labors nine months later. The other counsel were Mr. Waite, now Chief-Justice of the Supreme Court of the United States, and William M. Evarts. In 1873 he published a volume entitled "The Treaty of Washington," in which he sharply criticises the character and conduct of Sir Alexander Cockburn, the British arbitrator. This work, though written in his seventy-fourth year, shows no decline of mental power in the author.

The death of Chief-Justice Chase, in the spring of 1873, created a vacancy in the highest judicial office in the country. At the close of the year President Grant sought to have the office filled by the appointment of General Cushing, but the Senate evinced so much reluctance to confirming the nomination that he declined it. Soon afterward he was nominated and confirmed as Minister to Spain, our relations with which had become exceedingly critical, owing to circumstances that grew out of the Cuban insurrection. Assuming this arduous post in his seventy-fifth year, Mr. Cushing discharged his duties with ability and fidelity, and to the entire satisfaction of the appointing power and also of his country. He arrived home in April, 1877, and from that time until his death, which occurred at Newburyport, January 2d, 1879, enjoyed a well-earned rest, his intellect remaining unclouded to the last.

Notwithstanding Caleb Cushing's prominent and successful career, extending as it did for over half a century, and embracing all branches of political life, he was never popular. Neither the Whig nor the Republican party really liked him, and he was still further from being a favorite with the Democrats.

SARGEANT S. PRENTISS.

Sargeant Smith Prentiss was born at Portland, Maine, on the 30th day of September, 1810. He received a classical education at Bowdoin College, and at the age of about eighteen years he went to Mississippi, where, in the vicinity of Natchez, he spent two years as tutor in a private family and in the pursuit of legal studies, under the instruction of General Felix Houston.

Mr. Prentiss was always remarkable, from boyhood, for fluency of language and ready wit, and his first speech to a jury, after being admitted to the bar, won for him the highest applause from judges, colleagues, and opponents.

He made Vicksburg (then a small village) his residence in 1830, and he soon became the acknowledged head of his profession in that region. His eloquence was of that popular order which always charms and overpowers, and, like O'Connell, he could adapt his words and figures to his particular audience with wonderful facility. His practice became very lucrative, and the payment of his fee, in land, for his successful management of a suit which involved the most valuable portion of Vicksburg, made him, in a short time, one of the wealthiest men in the State.

Mr. Prentiss entered the field of politics with great enthusiasm, and was a brilliant and successful stump orator ; but at about the time his fellow-citizens called him to serve in the national councils he became embarrassed during the financial troubles of 1836, and removed to New Orleans, to retrieve his fortune by professional labor.

He first became known to the people of the United States in general when, in 1837, he appeared in the House of Representatives as a claimant of a disputed seat there. His speech in favor of his claim was listened to with the most profound attention, and it was admitted by all that he had no superior in the country as an eloquent and logical parliamentary debater. His claim was rejected by the casting vote of the Speaker, Mr. Polk, and he was sent back to the people. He at once canvassed the State, and was re-elected by an overwhelming majority.

His services in the House of Representatives were brief, but brilliant in the extreme.

Private engagements and a distaste for political life, produced by his discovery of its hollowness and its dangers, caused him to refuse office, and with great industry he applied himself to his profession in New Orleans. He was eminently successful. No man ever possessed greater powers of fascination by his forensic oratory than he, and few jurors could withstand that power.

Nor was he entirely absorbed in professional duties. He was distinguished for his love and knowledge of literature, and he was always prominent in philanthropic movements in the chosen city of his residence. His social qualities were of the highest order, and the attachment of his friends was exceedingly strong.

In the heat of his active career, and bearing the blossoms of greatest promise, he was suddenly stricken with disease, and died at Longwood, near Natchez, on the 1st of July, 1850.

PRESIDENT VAN BUREN'S CABINET.

Secretary of State.—John Forsyth, of Georgia, continued.
Secretary of the Treasury.—Levi Woodbury, of New Hampshire, continued.

Secretary of War.—Joel R. Poinsett, of South Carolina, appointed March 7th, 1837.

Secretaries of the Navy.—Mahlon Dickerson, of New Jersey, continued; James K. Paulding, of New York, appointed June 30th, 1838.

Postmasters-General.—Amos Kendall, of Kentucky, continued; John M. Niles, of Connecticut, appointed May 25th, 1840.

Attorneys-General.—Benjamin F. Butler, of New York, continued; Felix Grundy, of Tennessee, appointed September 1st, 1838; Henry D. Gilpin, of Pennsylvania, appointed January 10th, 1840.

Daniel Dougherty.

CHAPTER XIV.

CAMPAIGN OF 1840.

WHIG NOMINEES.

For President.
WILLIAM H. HARRISON of Ohio.

For Vice-President.
JOHN TYLER of Virginia.

DEMOCRATIC NOMINEES.

For President.
MARTIN VAN BUREN of New York.

For Vice-President.
RICHARD M. JOHNSON of Kentucky.

CONVENTIONS AND NOMINATIONS.

THE Whigs met in national convention at Harrisburg on the 4th of December, 1839, and selected as their candidates for President and Vice-President General William H. Harrison and General John Tyler.

The Democratic party assembled in national convention at Baltimore on the 5th of May, 1840, and unanimously nominated Martin Van Buren for President. The convention left the selection of a Vice-President to the States.

On November 13th, 1839, the Abolition party, which grew out of the *National Anti-Slavery Society*, held a convention at Warsaw, New York, and nominated James G. Birney, of Michigan, for President, and Francis I. Lemoyne, of Pennsylvania, for Vice-President. These nominees both declined, and the organization, in 1840, merged into the *Liberty Party*, and this latter party, at a convention subsequently held at Buffalo, nominated James G. Birney for President and Thomas Earle for Vice-President.

The canvass of 1840 marks a new era in the manner of conducting Presidential campaigns. Every possible means was employed to arouse popular enthusiasm. Mass meetings and processions were now first brought into use. The slur which had been cast upon Harrison that he lived in a "log cabin," with nothing to drink but "hard cider," was utilized as an electioneering appeal. Log cabins became a regular feature in political processions, and "hard cider" one of the watchwords of the party.

The result of the election gave General Harrison 234 electoral votes against 60 for Van Buren.

THOMAS CORWIN.

Thomas Corwin was born in Bourbon County, Kentucky, July 29th, 1794.

His father, Matthias Corwin, four years later removed with his family to what was then the North-western Territory, and settled near where Lebanon, Ohio, is now located.

Thomas Corwin was reared on a farm, where he was kept at hard labor, except in the winter months, when he studied at school or at home, as circumstances permitted. With limited opportunities he acquired much solid information.

In 1815 he commenced the study of law, and was admitted to the bar three years later. Corwin was a marvellous man, and no American of his time had higher claims to the title of orator than he.

His name bore magic to every one who had heard him speak, and the impression which he stamped upon an auditor was one of the enduring marks which the memory is last to surrender.

Very early in life he began to display his unusual powers. His strong phrases and vivid descriptions soon spread beyond the range of his own circle, and every inhabitant of Turtle Creek Valley felt pride in Tom Corwin.

In 1830 he made his first stump speech at Petersburg, in Highland County. The gentleman who rode over with him from Wilmington, and who heard the speech, remembers it as rather a *sober* effort, except the conclusion. "My speech," impressively said the young orator, "is now ended. No doubt you are all excessively weary. I can say, most conscientiously (placing his right hand solemnly upon his bosom and betraying a good deal of that facial power for which he afterward became so famous), that I am; and my mouth is as dry as a powder-horn. I propose that we adjourn, without further ceremony, to Captain Jessup's, and refresh ourselves. I can certify to the high qualities of the article he keeps."

In 1840 he made a famous speech in reply to Crary, of Michigan, who had attacked the military reputation of General Harrison, which gave him a national reputation. The next day after its delivery John Quincy Adams referred to the vanquished gentleman "as the late Mr. Crary, of Michigan."

The Whigs of Ohio made him their candidate for governor the same year, and during that canvass he rose to the zenith of his great popularity. For more than a hundred days, at as many different places, he spoke from two to three hours to great out-door assemblages, swaying them as he willed by his magical oratory. Never was man more completely the idol of the people. They pressed round him, and triumphantly carried him on their shoulders. They hung entranced upon every sentence which he uttered. Every day as he grew in favor he increased in intellectual stature, until it seemed the possibilities of his genius had no limit.

Notwithstanding such opportunities for training in the great art of popular eloquence—more powerful than any other in a people's government—few indeed who aspired to pre-eminence proved themselves possessed of the rare qualities essential, that would always bear the test, always meet expectation, and never weary. Corwin was one of the few and the chief. His voice was as clear as a silver bell, and attuned to the sweetest melody. In gesture he was as graceful and forcible as forest trees bowing before an approaching storm.

He knew the power of action, and, like Roscius, could express by gesture every variety of emotion and passion. In the Harrison campaign of 1840, a gentleman, among forty thousand others, was listening to one of Corwin's great speeches. Beside him was a man as deaf as the stump on which the orator figuratively stood, in breathless attention, apparently catching every word. Now the tears of delight would roll down his cheeks, and again, in ungovernable ecstasy, he would shout out applauses of the most vehement nature.

At length the speaker launched out one of those passages of massive declamation for which he was so distinguished. Its effect upon the multitude was like a whirlwind. The deaf man could contain himself no longer, but yelled into the bystander's ear, "Who's that a-speaking?" "Tom Corwin," replied the gentleman, as loud as his lungs would permit. "Who?" inquired the deaf man, still louder than before. "Tom Corwin," replied the gentleman, almost renting his throat in the effort. "Well, well," continued the afflicted man, "I can't hear a word he or you are saying; but, great Jackson, don't he do the motions splendid!"

Speakers of that period were frequently interrupted, and many amusing colloquies occurred. Corwin was ever ready for a reply, and a person who had once been answered seldom ventured a second question. On one occasion, during the campaign above referred to, some one interrupted the great orator and asked, "How can it be possible that so much trouble and hard times exist, and yet the men we have elected to office never whisper a word about it?"

Corwin's droll features began working, the very sight of which, before he had said a word, brought forth the audible smiles of the multitude.

"Fellow-citizens," said he, in deliberate tones, "I ever allude to the Holy Scriptures with deepest reverence, and on occasions like the present but seldom; but that venerable patriarch, Job, has so completely unravelled the difficulty of my honest opponent, that I must trespass to quote his words: 'Doth a wild beast bray while he hath grass, or loweth the ox over his fodder?'"

Two years later Corwin was again nominated for governor. Every one knew he would be elected, and hence no particular need of his leaving home to vote. This feeling pervaded the whole State, and great was the astonishment when the returns showed their idol was defeated. A farmer went to Lebanon to apologize for his dereliction of duty, and offered as an excuse the threatening weather, which he thought might catch his grain. "Yes," said Corwin, "that is the way with you farmers; and to save a little buckwheat you lost the best governor Ohio ever had."

Corwin knew the world, and seemed to see quite through the deeds of men. His quick sympathies took up every phase of life and made it his own.

To his great heart, perhaps it may be said, he owed his greatness more than to his great intellect.

The career of this brilliant orator closed in the city of Washington on the 18th day of December, 1865.

WILLIAM PITT FESSENDEN.

Unlike many of the public leaders during the anti-slavery and war era, William Pitt Fessenden was of gentle birth and university education. His father was a distinguished Maine lawyer. The son was graduated from Bowdoin College in 1823, when only seventeen years of age. Four years later he was admitted to the bar, and began practice in Bridgton, Maine, removing in 1829 to Portland. At the age of twenty-five he entered public life as the youngest member of the Maine Legislature, and showed great skill as a debater. He did not return to that body for seven years, devoting himself in the mean time to his profession, in which he rose to eminence. When thirty-five years of age he was elected to Congress as a Whig, served one term, and declined a renomination. His speech on the Loan and Bankrupt Bills are said to have created a good impression in Congress.

During the next ten years he was in the State Legislature two terms, was twice a candidate for United States Senator, and a member of several national conventions. In 1854 a union of Whigs and Free-Soil Democrats in the Maine Legislature sent him to the United States Senate. This was the birth of the Republican party in that State, and Mr. Fessenden was one of its greatest exponents.

It is unusual for a Senator to rise to eminence during his first session in that august body. Mr. Fessenden took his seat on February 23d, 1854. Within a fortnight he made a speech against the Nebraska bill, which was so eloquent that he at once became a leader among the Senators. In this speech he asserted that the South had already received her dues in the slavery contest, and that the present dissension was due to a desire on the part of the South to rob the North of the little left her. A number of notable speeches were afterward made by him, among them a severe review of President Buchanan's message on the Kansas question. He was returned to the Senate in 1859, and throughout the war supported the cause of the Union with his eloquence and logic. He was chairman of the Finance Committee, and hence had an important part to play in maintaining the nation's credit. It is said that as a general debater he was without a superior; he had wit, ready knowledge, and sarcasm to annoy his enemies. He was a careful legislator and a practical statesman.

One of his notable speeches was made in 1862, in advocacy of a bill to provide for the employment of negro soldiers. In the course of his address he said: "I tell the President, from my place here as Senator, and I tell the generals of our army they must reverse their practices and their course of proceeding on this subject. I advise it, here from my place—treat your enemies as enemies—as the worst of enemies—and avail yourselves like men of every power which God has placed in your hands to accomplish your purpose, within the rules of civilized warfare."

As Secretary of the Treasury, from July 5th, 1864, to March 4th, 1865, he restored the faith of the people in the ability of the Government to meet its obligations, and during that time gold fell from a premium of 185 to 99.

He re-entered the Senate in 1865. During the impeachment trial of Andrew Johnson Senator Fessenden surprised his friends and constituents by voting for acquittal. He made an elaborate defence of his course, in which he said that it was too grave a matter in which to yield to popular clamor or party spirit. He was everywhere condemned, but his well-known integrity and his efforts for the triumph of the Republican party in the election of General Grant, caused a reaction in his favor.

When he died, in 1869, the *Nation* said of him: "Senator Fessenden is doubtless not to be called a great man, able as he was, nor a man of wide culture in any field; but he was a man who has left to his country the legacy of a character and a career as lofty as that of any American who ever led a public life."

PRESIDENT HARRISON'S CABINET.

Secretary of State.—Daniel Webster, of Massachusetts, appointed March 5th, 1841.

Secretary of the Treasury.—Thomas Ewing, of Ohio, appointed March 5th, 1841.

Secretary of War.—John Bell, of Tennessee, appointed March 5th, 1841.

Secretary of the Navy.—George E. Badger, of North Carolina, appointed March 5th, 1841.

Postmaster-General.—Francis Granger, of New York, appointed March 6th, 1841.

Attorney-General.—John J. Crittenden, of Kentucky, appointed March 5th, 1841.

President Tyler continued all the Cabinet appointments made by President Harrison until their successors were appointed as follows :

PRESIDENT TYLER'S CABINET.

Secretaries of State.—Hugh S. Legaré, of South Carolina, appointed May 9th, 1843 ; Abel P. Upshur, of Virginia, appointed June 24th, 1843 ; John C. Calhoun, of South Carolina, appointed March 6th, 1844.

Secretaries of the Treasury.—Walter Forward, of Pennsylvania, appointed September 13th, 1841 ; George M. Bibb, of Kentucky, appointed June 15th, 1844.

Secretaries of War.—John C. Spencer, of New York, appointed October 12th, 1841 ; William Wilkins, of Pennsylvania, appointed February 15th, 1844.

Secretaries of the Navy.—Abel P. Upshur, of Virginia, appointed September 13th, 1841 ; David Henshaw, of Massachusetts, appointed July 24th, 1843 ; Thomas W. Gilmer, of Virginia, appointed February 15th, 1844 ; John T. Mason, of Virginia, appointed March 14th, 1844.

Postmaster-General.—Charles A. Wickliffe, of Kentucky, appointed September 13th, 1841.

Attorneys-General.—Hugh S. Legaré, of South Carolina, appointed September 13th, 1841 ; John Nelson, of Maryland, appointed January 2d, 1844.

CHAPTER XV.

CAMPAIGN OF 1844.

DEMOCRATIC NOMINEES.

For President.
JAMES K. POLK of Tennessee.

For Vice-President.
GEORGE M. DALLAS of Pennsylvania.

WHIG NOMINEES.

For President.
HENRY CLAY of Kentucky.

For Vice-President.
THEODORE FRELINGHUYSEN of New Jersey.

CONVENTIONS AND NOMINATIONS.

THE Democratic National Convention met at Baltimore on the 27th of May, and nominated James K. Polk and Silas Wright. Mr. Wright declined the nomination, and George M. Dallas was subsequently chosen.

The Whigs met in national convention at Baltimore on the 1st of May, and selected Clay and Frelinghuysen. This ticket was received with great enthusiasm.

The Liberty party met in national convention at Buffalo, New York, the 30th of August, 1843, and presented as candidates James G. Birney, of Michigan, and Thomas Morris, of Ohio.

James K. Polk at this election received 170 electoral votes against 105 for Henry Clay.

LEWIS CASS.

The name of Lewis Cass bears a distinctive impress upon the politics of his country. For more than half a century he was a prominent figure in public affairs, and during that time he made his name synonymous with pure integrity and indomitable courage. He was born at Exeter, New Hampshire, October 9th, 1782, and died in Detroit, Michigan, June 17th, 1866. In 1800 his father, Major Cass, removed to Marietta, Ohio, where Lewis studied law. In 1802 he was admitted to the bar, and began to practise in Zanesville.

In 1806 he was elected a member of the State Legislature, and in this capacity he drew the address to Jefferson, embodying the views of the Legislature on Aaron Burr's expedition, and drafted the law under which Burr's boats and provisions, built and collected in Ohio, were seized.

From 1807 to 1813 he was State marshal, and in the War of 1812 he was colonel of the Third Ohio Volunteers, under General Hull, and after Hull's surrender was appointed colonel of the Twenty-seventh Infantry, and was shortly afterward promoted to the rank of brigadier-general. At the close of the war he was in command of Michigan, and was appointed governor of the Territory. In 1831 President Jackson appointed him Secretary of War, and he was at the head of the War Department during the first two years of the Florida War, 1835-36. In 1836 he was sent as Minister to France. The most marked incident of his diplomatic career was his attack on the quintuple treaty for the suppression of the slave trade, which led to his resignation in 1842. In January, 1845, he was elected United States Senator from Michigan, which place he resigned on his nomination for the Presidency at the Baltimore Convention on the 22d of May, 1848. Mr. Cass was a prominent candidate at the Democratic National Convention, held four years before in the same city, when James K. Polk was the nominee.

A division in the Democratic party in New York gave the election to General Taylor in 1848, and in June, 1849, Mr. Cass was re-elected to the Senate.

In the Democratic Convention held in Baltimore in 1852 he was again a prominent candidate for the Presidency, and was supported by his friends with a zeal rarely accorded a candidate in any convention. Franklin Pierce, a name which had not before been mentioned, was introduced on the thirty-fifth ballot, and on the forty-ninth ballot he received a majority of votes over General Cass, and was made the nominee of the convention.

When General Cass left a convention without the honor of a nomination, he went forth to give his successful rival his earnest support. In 1844 he took the *stump*, and traversed Michigan, Indiana, Ohio, Tennessee, and Kentucky, urging the people, with argument and eloquence, to cast their votes for Polk and Dallas, as in 1852 he proclaimed for Pierce and King. In 1856 he was not a Presidential candidate, and warmly concurred in the nomination of Mr. Buchanan, and advocated his election with more than his usual zeal.

On Mr. Buchanan's accession to the Presidency, in 1857, he appointed Mr. Cass Secretary of State. In December, 1860, when Buchanan refused to re-enforce Major Anderson and reprovision Fort Sumter, he promptly resigned, and closed an honorable public career of fifty-four years.

DANIEL S. DICKINSON.

Daniel Stevens Dickinson was born in Goshen, Litchfield County, Connecticut, September 11th, 1800. Six years later his parents removed to the town of Oxford, Chenango County, New York, where he resided until 1831, when he made Binghamton, New York, his home.

From boyhood he was a leader in everything of a public nature, his talents and tastes peculiarly adapting him to take a foremost place in the ranks. Being once asked if in his youth he had any idea of the prominence he might attain in maturer years, he replied that there were then times when his imagination presented to him pictures of vast throngs, which he seemed to be addressing. That kind of public oratory now popularly known as "stump speaking" was not much in vogue in the region of country where he resided, before the Presidential campaigns of 1840 and 1844, personal appeals then being the more common medium through which matters of political interest were presented.

Identifying himself in the early part of his career with the Democratic party, he was, in the divisions which from time to time characterized it, "Hunker," "Hard Shell," and "War Democrat"—a most zealous exponent of the principles in which he believed.

WILLIAM M. EVARTS.

Mr. Dickinson had the happy gift of adapting his speeches, with felicitous tact, to occasion and circumstance. They were made with few and scanty notes, thus largely possessing the charm of spontaneity. He rarely wrote them out or even saw the reporter's copy until it appeared in print. If extemporaneous effort was called for, he was never surprised into a loss of self-possession nor failed to handsomely meet the emergency.

His style was delightfully varied, and while facts were clearly and forcibly laid before his audience, they were embellished by original metaphors, amusing anecdotes, pertinent quotations, and strains of glowing eloquence. His wit was diamond-bright, his humor irresistible, his pathos moving, his sarcasm keen and penetrating. He held a magic wand with which he could touch the hearts of his hearers, making them weep or laugh at his pleasure.

His mind was richly stored with treasures of poetry and prose, from which he made swift and apt selection as his subject might demand, and was always ready in sparkling repartee. His frequent illustrations and citations from Holy Writ indicated his familiarity with the pages of divine inspiration, and gained for him the *sobriquet* of "Scripture Dick."

His figure was erect, his countenance animated and genial, his voice pleasing and resonant, his manners extremely winning, and he possessed, in a marked degree, that personal magnetism which insures to a speaker great power over his audience.

He was very fond of little children ; his heart was full of tenderness for them. On one occasion, when in the midst of a speech which Mr. Dickinson was making, the crying of a child in the great assemblage came in as an *obligato* to the speaker's voice. Some incensed hearers called for a speedy removal of the young offender ; but Mr. Dickinson, advancing nearer the edge of the platform, requested that the little one might remain ; that patience should be exercised ; and paid a brief but telling and beautiful tribute to maternal love. It is needless to say that the mother's embarrassment, from being so conspicuously brought into notice, was largely mitigated by the orator's kindly and reassuring words.

Those conversant with the idiosyncrasies of New York State politics will remember the bitter feud between the "Hard" and "Soft" wings of the Democratic party. Realizing the necessity of *uniting forces* in order to insure success, Mr. Dickinson used his earnest influence to effect this desired result, but it proved unavailing. Alluding to this failure in a speech made by him at Cooper Institute, New York, July 18th, 1860, Mr. Dickinson, stung by what he deeply felt to be the treachery of the "Softs," indignantly declared that he would make no further exertion to secure a union with them, and quoted, with much feeling :

> "Twice have I sought Clan-Alpine's glen
> In peace ; but when I come again,
> I come with banner, brand, and bow,
> As leader seeks his mortal foe!"

Mr. Dickinson's speeches delivered during the war before great concourses, and upon a topic of such vital interest, are probably the best specimens of his popular oratory. A devoted lover of the Union, believing, with all his heart, in its preservation, his voice was heard throughout the land—a clarion call to duty, patriotism, and loyalty. Party interests to him were but as "sounding brass and tinkling cymbals" compared to the magnitude of the matter at stake, and he engaged in the work with all the earnestness and enthusiasm of his nature.

Mr. Dickinson was greatly beloved by a world-wide circle of friends, and even his sharpest political antagonists respected him for his honest worth—his pure and unblemished character. He was a devoted husband, an ideal father, a faithful friend. In this latter character his sincerity and truth were thoroughly tested ; for in his fidelity to Lewis Cass Mr. Dickinson declined the proud honor which, at the Baltimore Convention of 1852, seemed within his grasp.

Mr. Dickinson passed away, after a brief illness, in New York City, April 12th, 1866. Said the late lamented and scholarly Lyman Tremaine, in his eloquent oration delivered at the dedication of the monument to Mr. Dickinson in Spring Forest Cemetery, Binghamton, May 30th, 1872 : "It is believed that some passages in Mr. Dickinson's speeches, for splendid diction and beautiful imagery, will compare favorably with the finest specimens of ancient and modern oratory."

But anything approximating a just idea of Mr. Dickinson's great versatility of oratorical talent is prevented by the limited proportions of this volume. Therefore, from his numerous speeches, space can only be given for the following extract, taken from the one made by him at the memorable Union Mass Meeting held in Union Square, New York, April 20th, 1861 :

"For myself, in our federal relations, I know but one section, one Union, one flag, one Government. That section embraces every State ; that Union is the Union sealed with the blood and consecrated by the tears of the revolutionary struggle ; that flag is the flag known and honored in every sea under heaven, which has borne off glorious victory from many a bloody battle-field, and yet stirs with warmer and quicker pulsations the heart's blood of every true American, when he looks upon its Stars and Stripes wherever it waves. That Government is the Government of Washington, and Adams, and Jefferson, and Jackson ; a Government which has shielded and protected not only us, but God's oppressed children, who have gathered under its wings from every portion of the globe ; a Government which, from humble beginnings, has borne us forward with fabulous celerity, and made us one of the great and prosperous powers of earth. The Union of these States was a bright vision of my early years, the pride of my manhood, the ambition of my public service. I have sacrificed upon its altar the best energies and choicest hopes of a life checkered by vicissitudes and trial. I had believed the contemplation of its beauties would be the companion of approaching age and the beguiler of my vacant and solitary hours. And now that its integrity is menaced, its fair proportions disfigured, it is still dear to my heart, as a great fountain of wisdom, from which incalculable blessings have flowed. I have rejoiced with it in its heyday of success and triumph, and will, by the grace of God, stand by it in its hour of darkness and peril, and by those who uphold it in the spirit of the Constitution. When the timid falter and the faithless fly—when the skies lower, the winds howl, the storm descends, and the tempests beat—when the lightnings flash, the thunders roar, the waves dash, and the good ship Union creaks and groans with the expiring throes of dissolution, I will cling to her still as the last refuge of hope from the fury of the storm ; and if she goes down I will go down with her, rather than survive to tell the story of her ignoble end. I will sustain that flag of Stars and Stripes, recently made more glorious by Anderson, his officers, and men, wherever it waves—over the sea or over the land. And when it shall be despoiled and disfigured, I will rally around it still as the star-spangled banner of my fathers and my country ; and so long as a single stripe can be discovered, or a single star shall glimmer from the surrounding darkness, I will cheer it as the emblem of a nation's glory and a nation's hope !"

THOMAS MARSHALL.

As an orator, Tom Marshall was the foremost Kentuckian of his time, and, for that matter, of any time, since his time included the first orators Kentucky has produced—Clay, Barry, Pope, Rowan, Bledsoe, Menefee, the Breckenridges, and the other Marshalls, some of them only less eloquent than their peerless kinsman. Yet he made so slight an impression on his time, so few are the recorded products of his genius, and so much of his fame arose from popular efforts, which perished in the delivery, as, in truth, the wonder-working power of all oratory must needs perish, that his name will live chiefly in tradition.

Mr. Marshall was born in Frankfort, Kentucky, June 7th, 1801. His father, Dr. Lewis Marshall, himself a man of fine intellect, was the youngest brother of Chief-Justice Marshall. His mother also was a person of remarkable mind as well as remarkable beauty; so he came honestly by his intellectual gifts. Like Mill, Spencer, Buckle, and others of the best-trained intellects of the race, young Marshall was educated at home, never seeing the inside of a university or college.

In 1829, as the guest of Justice Marshall, at Richmond, Virginia, he attended the debates of the Constitutional Convention, listening to Madison, Monroe, Randolph, Leigh, and their compeers, returning home by Washington in time to hear the great debate between Hayne and Webster.

In 1832 he was elected by the Whigs of the county of Woodford to the Lower House of the Legislature, where he at once distinguished himself, not only as a brilliant speaker, but as a sound and clear thinker.

The following year he removed to Louisville, resolved to pursue his profession; but this resolution was soon broken, for Louisville sent him to the Legislature at the very next election, and at the succeeding one.

In 1837, still a resident of Louisville, he stood for Congress as an independent candidate, in opposition to William J. Graves, the Whig candidate, and was defeated. Marshall, so accustomed to victory, did not take his defeat with humility, but returned to Woodford, whence, for the next two years, he was sent without opposition to the Legislature.

In 1841 he was, without opposition, elected to Congress from the Ashland District. His career in Congress was short, but uncommonly brilliant. One of his speeches was on distribution, which John Quincy Adams pronounced the ablest speech he had heard on the subject, although he had just heard Mr. Clay. One other speech of his has come down to us from that day—a temperance speech, delivered in the Hall of Representatives, before the Congressional Total Abstinence Society, formed, it seems, for the reformation of Congressional inebriates, of whom our subject was reputed one, though in his speech he protested, with characteristic humor, that his inebriety was not habitual. "I had earned," he said, "a most unenviable notoriety by excesses, which, though bad enough, did not half reach the reputation they won for me. I never was an habitual drunkard. I was one of your spreeing gentry. My sprees, however, began to crowd each other so fast that my best friends feared that they would soon run together."

He had great contempt for the administration of Tyler, declaring that when the history of the country was written the Tyler administration might be put in a parenthesis, which he defined from Lindley Murray as "a clause of a sentence inclosed between black lines, or brackets, which should be pronounced in a low tone of voice, and which might be left out altogether without injuring the sense."

Mr. Marshall fought, during this time, a duel with James Watson Webb. Webb was shot below the knee-joint, prompting Marshall to cry out on the spot, "It is the lowest act of my life." Marshall, in the course of his life, fought two other duels, one with a son of Judge Rowan, of Kentucky, the other with James S. Jackson, being fought while both were serving in the Mexican War.

Marshall, among his other adventures in Mexico, had a difficulty with Cassius M. Clay. Marshall was one day walking, unarmed, through camp, when Clay stepped to his tent-door and completely covered him with a pistol. Marshall instantly turned his back, and looking over his shoulder at Clay, said, "Shoot away, Cash, but it's got to be a clear case of murder."

In 1845 Marshall ran for Congress against Garrett Davis, by whom he was beaten, and in 1850, the Mexican War having broken out, he raised a company of cavalry, of which he was chosen captain, and which he led to the theatre of war. On his return he spent much of his time in Lexington, where his friend and kinsman, Dr. Robert J. Breckenridge, was settled as pastor of the First Presbyterian Church. For several years they had been members of the same bar, which, according to Marshall, they had both rather suddenly forsaken, "Bob," as he used to say, "taking to the Bible, and I to the bottle; and the world says I have stuck to my text a good deal closer than he has to his."

118   THE LEADING ORATORS OF TWENTY-FIVE CAMPAIGNS.

In 1851 he again represented Woodford County in the Legislature. With this term Marshall's career as a Legislator closed. In the civil war he took no part. His life's work was nearly done, and his death soon followed. Shortly before his death he met Dr. Breckenridge, and said to him : " I have read your book, ' God Objectively Considered,' and I am glad to find you have no objection to God." " As one of His vice gerents on earth, I can tell you He has very great objections to you," retorted Breckenridge, and went his way.

Tom Marshall died on the 22d of September, 1864, leaving a wife, but no children and no fortune. He lived and died poor. He left to posterity nothing but the fading memory of his genius.

PRESIDENT POLK'S CABINET.

Secretary of State.—James Buchanan, of Pennsylvania, appointed March 6th, 1845.

Secretary of the Treasury.—Robert I. Walker, of Mississippi, appointed March 6th, 1845.

Secretary of War.—William L. Marcy, of New York, appointed March 5th, 1845.

Secretaries of the Navy.—George Bancroft, of Massachusetts, appointed March 10th, 1845 ; John T. Mason, of Virginia, appointed September 9th, 1846.

Postmaster-General.—Carr Johnson, of Tennessee, appointed March 5th, 1845.

Attorneys-General.—John T. Mason, of Virginia, appointed March 5th, 1845 ; Nathan Clifford, of Maine, appointed December 23d, 1846 ; Isaac Toucey, of Connecticut, appointed June 21st, 1848.

CHAPTER XVI.

CAMPAIGN OF 1848.

WHIG NOMINEES.

For President.
ZACHARY TAYLOR of Louisiana.

For Vice-President.
MILLARD FILLMORE of New York.

DEMOCRATIC NOMINEES.

For President.
LEWIS CASS of Michigan.

For Vice-President.
WILLIAM O. BUTLER of Kentucky.

FREE-SOIL NOMINEES.

For President.
MARTIN VAN BUREN of New York.

For Vice-President.
CHARLES FRANCIS ADAMS of Massachusetts

CONVENTIONS AND NOMINATIONS.

THE Liberty party again met in national convention at Buffalo, in October, 1847, and nominated John P. Hale, of New Hampshire, and Leicester King.

The Liberty League, organized in 1845, met in convention at Auburn, New York, in January, 1848, and nominated Gerrit Smith, of New York, and Elihu Burritt, of Massachusetts. Mr. Burritt declined, and C. C. Foote, of Michigan, was selected.

The Democratic National Convention convened at Baltimore on the 22d of May, and nominated General Lewis Cass and William O. Butler.

The Whig party met in national convention at Philadelphia on the 7th of June, and nominated General Zachary Taylor and Millard Fillmore.

The Free-Soil party held its first convention in Buffalo, on the 9th of August, and nominated Martin Van Buren for President and Charles Francis Adams for Vice-President.

The Liberty party withdrew the nominations which it had previously made, joined in the proceedings of this convention and identified itself with this new party in principles and name.

This election gave General Taylor 163 electoral votes against 127 for Lewis Cass.

HENRY WINTER DAVIS.

The subject of this sketch was born in Annapolis, Maryland, August 16th, 1817. His early education began at home under the supervision of his father, a clergyman of the Episcopal Church.

In 1837 he graduated at Kenyon College, Ohio, and in October, 1839, he entered the University of Virginia, where he pursued a thorough legal course, and laid the foundation of the elegant scholarship which distinguished him not less than his legal research and brilliant oratory.

After completing his legal studies he settled in Alexandria, Virginia, and shortly afterward removed to Baltimore. At this early period he was a frequent contributor to the newspapers on political subjects, many of which attracted wide attention.

In politics he was allied with the Whig party, and took an active part in the Scott campaign of 1852. On the defeat and final extinction of the Whigs, Mr. Davis adopted the principles of the American party. He was elected to a seat in the Thirty-fourth Congress in 1855, where he was continued several terms. In the House of Representatives he was soon recognized as one of its ablest debaters. He always commanded the attention of his auditors by his logical reasoning, his elegant array of facts, the chaste but fervid eloquence of his diction, the strength and melody of his voice,

RICHARD B. HUBBARD.

and his handsome and commanding presence. Mr. Davis was an ardent supporter of Mr. Fillmore for the Presidency in 1856 and Mr. Bell in 1860. Few men, as polished orators, have ranked higher than Henry Winter Davis. He died in Baltimore December 30th, 1864, in his forty-eighth year.

CHARLES SUMNER.

In 1837 a young lawyer of Boston, twenty-six years old, was described by the famous Judge Story as one " giving promise of the most eminent distinction in his profession, with extraordinary attainments, literary and judicial, and a gentleman of the highest purity and propriety of character." As a prediction of Charles Sumner's future, these words, remarkable as they were, fell short of his brilliant career ; as a tribute to his intellectual and moral worth, they fitly serve to voice a nation's verdict on one of her chief statesmen and scholars.

Born in Boston, Massachusetts, January 6th, 1811, of a stock owning generations of culture, Charles Sumner was fitted at the Boston Latin School for Harvard College. Graduating from the latter in 1830, he pursued his legal studies under Story, the master of constitutional law.

Fortified by this training, he visited England, France, and Germany in 1837, being received in each country with unusual distinction in the highest circles. The years thus passed abroad served to develop his understanding of the law of nations, to add materially to his worldly information and address, and to supplement his profound knowledge of the classics, with the acquisition of the chief modern languages and their literatures.

Returning to Boston in 1840, he at first took no active part in politics, though voting with the Whigs. Yet his family antecedents pointed him toward politics, his father having been High Sheriff of Suffolk County and a cousin of his father's a distinguished judge and Governor of the State. His studies and predilections pointed in the same direction ; and a tall form and commanding presence, a grace of manner and superb vitality, elegance of diction and force of ideas combined to insure him welcome as a public speaker. An occasion was needed, and it came. Prompted by the menacing aspect of affairs between the United States and Mexico, he delivered an oration on the 4th of July, 1845, before the municipal authorities of Boston, on " The True Grandeur of Nations," denouncing the practice of war and advocating international arbitration. This speech, circulated widely in America and Europe, and pronounced by Cobden one of the noblest contributions to the cause of peace, was followed in rapid succession by public addresses on kindred themes.

At length the great question of slavery engaged his attention, and led to his oration on "The Anti-Slavery Duties of the Whig Party," in which he declared himself the opponent of slavery on constitutional grounds. His watchword was, "Repeal of slavery under the Constitution and laws of the Federal Government." It was a bold and courageous step to take, for the "Brahmin caste of New England" promised to the youthful orator social and political death. But Mr. Sumner, loving the absolute right, a man of noble ideas and lofty enthusiasms, only increased his earnest opposition to slavery, and left the Whigs to join the Free-Soil party in 1848. Webster was in the United States Senate, and upon him Sumner called to earn for himself the title of "Defender of Humanity" by opposing the fugitive slave law. It was in vain; but the withdrawal of Mr. Webster into President Fillmore's Cabinet opened the way to Mr. Sumner's election to the Senate. He entered upon his duties as a Senator December 1st, 1851, and retained his seat in that capacity till his death, in 1874. In his first important speech in the Senate against the fugitive slave law, he uttered the famous political formula, "Freedom National, Slavery Sectional." Then came his speech on "The Crime against Kansas," March 19th and 20th, 1856, and the physical assault upon him by Preston S. Brooks. Under medical treatment, more or less, for the next three years, he returned to the charge in 1859 in another great speech—"The Barbarism of Slavery"—a speech singularly devoid of personal griefs, and alive only to the burning question of the day.

Upholding Lincoln and his administration, Mr. Sumner throughout the civil war opposed all compromise with the upholders of slavery. He early advocated emancipation, not only on moral and historical, but on constitutional grounds. As chairman of the Committee on Foreign Relations, he delivered an elaborate speech, January 9th, 1862, arguing that the seizure of Mason and Slidell was unjustifiable by international law. The speech went far to reconcile the public mind to the surrender of the Confederate envoys. Subsequent speeches on "Our Foreign Relations" (1863), "The Case of the Florida" (1864), a eulogy of President Lincoln (1865), on the Thirteenth Amendment and Reconstruction acts, "Our claims on England" (1869), and "Against the Santo Domingo Treaty"

(1869) sustained his reputation as a statesman and orator, though the last speech, by the offence it gave the Administration, caused his removal, in 1870, from the chairmanship of the Committee on Foreign Relations.

Supporting Mr. Greeley for the Presidency in 1872, he was nominated for Governor of Massachusetts by a convention of "Liberal Republicans" and Democrats, but he declined the nomination.

His last important public acts were an able speech regarding the sale of arms to France during the Franco-German War, the promotion of the Civil Rights bill, and a resolution to efface from the regimental colors of the army and from the army register the names of the battles won over fellow-citizens in the civil war. This last bill was strongly denounced, and led to a vote of censure on Mr. Sumner by the Massachusetts Legislature in 1873. It was rescinded, however, in 1874, just before his death, which occurred suddenly in Washington, March 11th, 1874.

As a thinker, Mr. Sumner was vigorous and comprehensive. There was a tendency in his mind to seek the ideal—he had a capacity for abstractions —principles were everything. Consistency marked his public life—the advocacy of peace in place of war principles in his oration in 1845, on "The True Grandeur of Nations," was the key-note that held through to his bill in 1874, calling for the erasure of the names of battles from regimental colors. His integrity of motive, lofty patriotism, and splendid intellectuality gained for him respectful attention and great influence.

As an orator he was polished, his arguments being re-enforced by historical and classical allusions in a very marked degree, though at times bordering on pedantry.

PRESIDENT TAYLOR'S CABINET.

Secretary of State.—John M. Clayton, of Delaware, appointed March 7th, 1849.

Secretary of the Treasury.—William M. Meredith, of Pennsylvania, appointed March 8th, 1849.

Secretary of War.—George W. Crawford, of Georgia, appointed March 6th, 1849.

Secretary of the Navy.—William B. Preston, of Virginia, appointed March 8th, 1849.

Secretary of the Interior.—Thomas Ewing, of Ohio, appointed March 7th, 1849.

Postmaster-General.—Jacob Collamer, of Vermont, appointed March 7th, 1849.

Attorney-General.—Reverdy Johnson, of Maryland, appointed March 7th, 1849.

The Cabinet officers appointed by President Taylor, who died July 9th, 1850, were all continued by President Fillmore until their successors were appointed, as follows:

Secretaries of State.—Daniel Webster, of Massachusetts, appointed July 20th, 1850; Edward Everett, of Massachusetts, appointed November 6th, 1852.

Secretary of the Treasury.—Thomas Corwin, of Ohio, appointed July 23d, 1850.

Secretary of War.—Charles M. Conrad, of Louisiana, appointed July 15th, 1850.

Secretaries of the Navy.—William A. Graham, of North Carolina, appointed July 22d, 1850; John P. Kennedy, of Maryland, appointed July 22d, 1852.

Secretary of the Interior.—Alexander H. H. Stuart, of Virginia, appointed July 22d, 1850.

Postmaster-General.—Nathan K. Hall, of New York, appointed July 20th, 1850; Samuel D. Hubbard, of Connecticut, appointed September 14th, 1852.

Attorney-General.—John J. Crittenden, of Kentucky, appointed July 20th, 1850.

CHAPTER XVII.

CAMPAIGN OF 1852

DEMOCRATIC NOMINEES.

For President.
FRANKLIN PIERCE of New Hampshire.

For Vice-President.
WILLIAM R. KING of Alabama.

WHIG NOMINEES.

For President
WINFIELD SCOTT of Virginia.

For Vice-President.
WILLIAM A. GRAHAM of North Carolina.

FREE-SOIL NOMINEES.

For President.
JOHN P. HALE of New Hampshire.

For Vice-President.
GEORGE W. JULIAN of Indiana.

CONVENTIONS AND NOMINATIONS.

THE Democratic party again met in convention at Baltimore on the 1st of June, 1852, and nominated Franklin Pierce and William R. King.

The Whigs held their convention on the 16th of June in the same city and nominated General Scott and William A. Graham.

The Free-Soil party met in national convention at Pittsburg, August 11th, and nominated John P. Hale, of New Hampshire, and George W. Julian, of Indiana, for the offices of President and Vice-President.

Two hundred and fifty-four electoral votes were cast for Franklin Pierce and 42 for General Scott.

HENRY WARD BEECHER.

Henry Ward Beecher, son of Lyman Beecher, a noted divine, was born in Litchfield, Connecticut, on the 24th of June, 1813. Mrs. Harriet Beecher Stowe, Mr. Beecher's sister, says, in a sketch of his life, that " Henry Ward was not marked out by the prophecies of partial friends for any brilliant future. He had precisely the organization which often passes for dulness in early boyhood. He had great deficiency in verbal memory ; he was excessively sensitive to praise and blame, extremely diffident, and with a power of yearning, undeveloped emotion, which he neither understood nor could express. His utterance was thick and indistinct, partly from bashfulness and partly from an enlargement of the tonsils of the throat, so that in speaking or reading he was with difficulty understood. In forecasting his horoscope—had any one taken the trouble then to do it —the last success that ever would have been predicted for him would have been that of an orator. ' When Henry is sent to me with a message,' said a good aunt, ' I always have to make him say it three times. The first time I have no manner of an idea more than if he spoke Choctaw ; the second, I catch now and then a word ; but the third time I begin to understand.' " From that indifferent beginning, Henry Ward Beecher developed into " the greatest pulpit orator since the days of Paul."

Young Beecher very early in life showed an inclination to defend good principles and opinions. " The stand he took in college was from the first that of a reformer. He was always on the side of law and order, and being one of the most popular fellows in his class, threw the whole weight of his popularity in favor of the faculty, rather than against them. He and his associates formed a union of merry good fellows, who were to have wholesome fun, but to have it only by honorable and permissible means. They voted down hazing of students ; they voted down gambling, and drinking, and every form of secret vice, and made the class rigidly temperate and pure.

"The only thing which prevented him from taking the first rank as a religious young man was the want of that sobriety and solemnity which was looked upon as essential to the Christian character.

"During his two last college years, Mr. Beecher taught rural schools during the long winter vacations. In the controversy then arising through the land in relation to slavery, Mr. Beecher from the first took the ground, and was willing to bear the name of an Abolitionist. It was a part of the heroic element of his nature always to stand for the weak, and he naturally inclined to take that stand in a battle where the few were at odds against the many."

Mr. Beecher graduated from Amherst College in 1834, and went to Cincinnati, whither his father, Dr. Lyman Beecher, had preceded him two years, and there entered upon the study of theology at Lane Seminary. Finishing his course at that institution, he settled at Lawrenceburg, and began the ministry in its broadest sense. His parish was a little town on the Ohio River. Here he preached in a small church, and did all the work of the parish sexton, making the fires, trimming the lamps, sweeping the church, and ringing the bell to call his congregation together. He said: "I did all but come to hear myself preach—that they had to do." Mr. Beecher was soon invited from Lawrenceburg to Indianapolis, where he labored for eight years.

In this new field Mr. Beecher pursued his theological studies with two volumes—the Bible and human nature. He was an intense observer and student of men, and no one knows his kind better. Every phase of human life is as familiar to him as "an open book."

In 1847 Mr. Beecher was invited to Brooklyn to take charge of Plymouth Church, and he immediately announced from that pulpit, to all whom it might concern, that he considered temperance and anti-slavery a part of the gospel of Christ, and should preach them accordingly. During the battle inaugurated by Webster's speech of the 7th of March and the fugitive slave law, Mr. Beecher preached and visited from store to store, holding up the courage of his people to resistance. At this time he carried this subject through New England and New York, in lyceum lectures, and began a course of articles in the *Independent*, which were widely read. It is said that when Calhoun was in his last illness, his secretary was reading him extracts from Northern papers, and, among others, one of Mr. Beecher's entitled "Shall we Compromise?" in which he fully set forth the utter impossibility of reconciling the two conflicting powers of 'reedom and slavery. "Read that again," said the old-statesman. "That fellow understands his subject; he has gone to the bottom of it."

When the battle of the settlement of Kansas was going on, Mr. Beecher fearlessly advocated the necessity of their going out armed, and a subscription was raised in his church to supply every family with a Bible and a rifle. During the war Mr. Beecher's labors were incessant and well chosen, and in his sphere of action no soldier of the Union did better or more valiant service.

In 1863 he visited Great Britain, with a special view to disabuse the public in regard to the issues of the civil war. His speeches in that behalf, delivered to vast assemblages in London, Liverpool, Manchester, Glasgow, and other cities, exerted a wide influence in changing popular sentiment, which had been strongly in favor of the Southern Confederacy. When the war was over, Mr. Beecher immediately advocated the benign doctrine of brotherly love and reconciliation between the sections, and his lead in that direction and visits to and ministry through the South, was one of the first-laid stepping-stones to reconstruction. Since the organization of the Republican party, Mr. Beecher has been one of its most consistent and steadfast supporters, and one of the most able and eloquent advocates of its principles.

SCHUYLER COLFAX.

Schuyler Colfax was born in the city of New York on the 23d of March, 1823. His father, who bore the same Christian name, was an officer of one of the New York City banks, and died four months before his son, the Speaker, was born. At the age of ten he had received all the school training which his widowed mother was able to provide him, and at that tender age he was placed in a store, to contribute what he could toward the family support. After three years he removed to Indiana with his mother and her second husband, a Mr. Matthews, and settled with them in St. Joseph County. Here young Colfax for four years again served as clerk in the village of New Carlisle, and when he had reached his eighteenth year he was appointed deputy county auditor; and for the better fulfilment of his official duties, he removed to the county town, South Bend, where he has lived ever since. Here, in this new position, he was enveloped in a political atmosphere which he imbibed freely. He talked and thought, and

HUGH JUDSON KILPATRICK.

began to print his views from time to time in the local newspapers of the place. He possessed a happy faculty of dealing fairly and at the same time pleasantly with every phase of a political question, and with all sorts of men; and his speeches and writings were regarded rather the impartial charge of a judge than the utterances of a partisan advocate. In 1845 he became proprietor and editor of the *St. Joseph Valley Register*, the local paper of South Bend. This was his first venture and if hope had been lacking the prospect would have foreboded a sorry future. He was a youth of just over twenty-one, and had but two hundred and fifty subscribers. But young Colfax had hope, and, what was far more important, remarkable tact and capacity for his laborious profession. At the end of the first year of his paper he was $1375 in debt. There is a peculiar fatality which ever hovers over such enterprises, and its blighting hand had reached out for young Colfax's journal; but with one hand he shielded it from the monster's grasp, and with the other he nurtured it to productive life. A few years afterward the office was burned down, and the uninsured editor was left to begin his business over again.

"Besides paying well, the *Register*, as conducted by Mr. Colfax, is entitled to the much higher praise of having been a useful, interesting, and a morally pure paper, always on the side of what is good and right in morals and in society."

Mr. Colfax was a Whig in the days of the Whig party, and on its dissolution he joined the Republican party. His first nomination for Congress was in 1851, and he was beaten, though only by two hundred majority, in a district strongly opposed to him in politics. In 1852 he was a delegate to the Whig National Convention that nominated General Scott, and was chosen secretary.

Mr. Colfax was chosen to the Thirty-fourth Congress by a large majority, and in that body he showed himself to be a judicious legislator, a ready debater, and a fine speaker. It was during this session that Mr. Colfax delivered his well-known and powerful speech on the bogus "Laws" of Kansas. This speech, a word-for-word quotation of clause after clause of this infamous code, accompanied with a plain, sober, and calmly-toned explanation of its provisions, produced a very great effect, and was considered so able a summary of the case involved that during the Presidential campaign of that year a half million copies of it were distributed among the voters of the United States.

On the 7th of December, 1863, Mr. Colfax was elected Speaker of the

Thirty-eighth Congress, and re-elected Speaker in 1865 and again in 1867.

In May, 1868, he was nominated at the Chicago National Republican Convention for Vice-President, with General Grant as candidate for President. This ticket was elected in November following, and on the 4th of March, 1869, he was inaugurated as Vice-President of the United States, and took his seat as President of the Senate. Failing in a renomination for the same office at the Philadelphia Convention in 1872, he retired to private life.

FREDERICK DOUGLASS.

On all the pages of history, there is not related the story of a life which is more eventful than that of Frederick Douglass.

He was born on Colonel Lloyd's plantation, at Tuckahoe, near Eaton, Talbot County, Maryland, about the year 1817. He says of his childhood days: "I was seldom whipped, and never severely, by my old master. I suffered little from any treatment I received, except from hunger and cold. In the heat of summer or cold of winter alike I was kept almost in a state of nudity—with nothing but a coarse tow-linen shirt reaching to the knee. This I wore night and day. In the daytime I could protect myself pretty well by keeping on the sunny side of the house, and in bad weather in the corner of the kitchen chimney. The great difficulty was to keep warm at night. I had no bed. The pigs in the pen had leaves, and horses in the stable had straw, but the children had nothing. In very cold weather I sometimes got down the bag in which corn was carried to the mill, and got into that. My feet have been so cracked by the frost that the pen with which I am writing might be laid in the gashes. Our corn-meal mush was placed in a large wooden trough, and the children were called; and like so many pigs they would come, and literally devour the mush. He that ate fastest got the most, and he that was strongest got the best place, and few left the trough really satisfied."

The effect of this on his childish mind is thus told: "As I grew older and more thoughtful I was more and more filled with a sense of my own wretchedness. The cruelty of my mistress, the hunger and cold I suffered, and the terrible reports of wrong and outrage that filled my ear, together with what I almost daily witnessed, led me, when I was but eight or nine years old, to wish I had never been born. I was just as well aware of the unjust, unnatural, and murderous character of slavery when nine years old as I am now. Without any appeal to books, to laws, or to authorities of any kind, it was enough to accept God as a Father, to regard slavery as a crime."

When Douglass was ten years of age a great change took place in his circumstances. His old master sent him to Baltimore to be a family servant in the house of a connection.

He speaks with great affection of his new mistress. She had never had to do with a slave child before, and seemed to approach him with all the tender feelings of motherhood. His clothing, lodging, and food were now those of a favorite servant. He begged his kind mistress to teach him to read, and he tells the result in his own words:

"The dear woman began the task, and very soon, by her assistance, I was master of the alphabet, and could spell words of three or four letters.

"My mistress seemed almost as proud of my progress as if I had been her own child, and supposing that her husband would be as well pleased, she made no secret of what she was doing for me. She told him of the aptness of her pupil and of her intention to persevere in teaching me. Her husband was amazed, and immediately made strenuous objections to the plan. He unfolded to her the true philosophy of slavery, and the peculiar rules necessary to be observed by masters and mistresses toward their human chattels.

"'Learning will spoil the best nigger in the world. If you learn him how to read he will want to know how to write, and this accomplished he will run away and leave you.'

"The effect of his words on me was neither slight nor transitory. His iron sentences, cold and harsh, sunk into my heart, and stirred up not only feelings of rebellion, but awakened within me a slumbering train of vital thought." The desire of learning once awakened could not be crushed, and although his mistress became jealously anxious to prevent him making further progress, he found means to continue the instruction. With a spelling-book hid away in his bosom he continued daily to get lessons from the street-boys whom he met while going on his errands. At last he made money enough to buy secretly a liberty-loving book called "The Columbian Orator." In its pages young Fred found most inspiring documents. He read the great speeches of Sheridan, Lord Chatham, William Pitt, Fox, and others, and added much to his limited knowledge of language.

All the results of learning to read predicted by his master came to pass.

He became morose and melancholy, and his mistress showered reproaches upon him. He soon began to acquire the art of writing, and studied how to form the letters from the painted signs on fences and bill-boards. He had various reverses as he grew in age and developed in manliness. He was found difficult to manage, and changed from hand to hand like a vicious horse. Finally his master made a virtue of necessity, and allowed him to hire his own time. He became a caulker in a shipyard, but the work was hard, and he determined to escape. He managed to reach New Bedford, Massachusetts, in safety, and there he took the name of Douglass. He married a thrifty and affectionate wife, and became a settled family man. He began to attend meetings of the colored people, and was amazed to hear them make speeches and to see them draw up resolutions.

He met William Lloyd Garrison, who took a friendly interest in the bright young colored man, and thence his course was upward. He attended an anti-slavery meeting in Nantucket, Massachusetts, in 1841, and related his experiences before a great audience. Douglass rapidly became an accomplished speaker and writer. He was offered the agency of the Massachusetts Anti-Slavery Society, which he accepted, and for four years he travelled and lectured throughout New England, meeting with astonishing success. Few men could mount a platform and deliver an unwritten speech with the cultured and moving eloquence of Fred Douglass. In 1845 he published his autobiography, recounting his slave days with touching pathos. Soon after he went to Europe, and lectured on the Continent with great effect. In 1847 he published a weekly paper in Boston, called the *North Star*. When the war broke out Douglass urged upon President Lincoln the employment of colored troops, and he greatly assisted in filling up those regiments. After the war he applied himself in lecturing for lyceums, and his oratory was heard all over the United States. He became editor of the *New National Era* in Washington, and in 1871 he was appointed secretary to the Commission to Santo Domingo. Later President Grant appointed him one of the Territorial Council of the District of Columbia. In 1872 he was elected a Presidential elector from New York State, and was appointed to carry the electoral vote of New York to Washington. Later on he was appointed marshal of the Supreme Court of the District of Columbia, a position of dignity and profit, which he held until President Garfield appointed him Register of the District.

A few months since Mr. Douglass married Miss Hannah Pitts, a representative of an intelligent and influential family of western New York.

ROBERT C. SCHENCK.

Robert C. Schenck was born at Franklin, Warren County, Ohio, in October, 1809. His father, General William C. Schenck, having emigrated from Huntington, Long Island, was one of the earliest settlers of the Miami Valley. Very early in life young Schenck showed promise of that ability to fight hard in a just cause, which afterward made him distinguished among American legislators.

In 1824 he entered Miami University at Oxford, Ohio, as a sophomore, and after three years of hard study he graduated, with the first honors of his class. In 1829 he commenced the study of law at Oxford, and subsequently entered the office of the distinguished orator and lawyer, "Tom" Corwin, with whom he finished his legal course. He was admitted to the bar in his twenty-first year.

With a sealed letter of introduction from Mr. Corwin, "To whom it might concern," he set out in quest of a location. He first went to Dayton, and presenting his letter to Hon. Joseph H. Crane, and that lawyer needing assistance, gave him a share in his business. With such a favorable start, he made rapid progress to eminence in his profession.

In 1838 he was made the Whig candidate for the Legislature, and made an active personal canvas; but despite every effort, he was defeated by a small majority. Three years later he again consented to become the Whig candidate for the same office, and was elected. At this time he had become known throughout his portion of the State as one of the ablest public speakers who discussed political or other questions. His style was particularly noticeable then, as in after years, for conciseness, clearness, vigor, and power of invective. There were not a few persons who held that in all these qualities he was the equal, if not the superior, of his great instructor, the renowned Thomas Corwin. This enviable reputation he had gained principally through his connection with the "log-cabin and hard cider campaign" of 1840.

General Harrison, the Whig candidate for the Presidency, he had known from boyhood, and it was a high compliment paid to his abilities at that time to receive an invitation from Harrison himself to take the stump in advocacy of the Whig cause. With Harrison, the Presidential candidate, and many other distinguished speakers he attended the memorable mass meeting held at Fort Meigs, and to this day it is recalled as one of the most remarkable political gatherings the county has ever known. From twenty-five to thirty thousand people came to attend it. They rode, walked, and drove in from all the country around, and camped out, lived in wagons, and slept upon the ground as they could, feeling themselves fully rewarded for all their trouble by the speeches of their candidate and his friends.

Arriving at the capital of Ohio after that election, he found that his reputation had gone before him, and that he was confidentially expected to assume the leadership of the Whigs in the Legislature. This responsibility he did not shirk, and so admirably did he manage the party's forces that he more than justified all estimates of him as a skilful leader. After Mr. Harrison's inauguration he tendered young Schenck the District Attorneyship of Ohio ; but this office he declined.

Mr. Schenck was returned to the Legislature the following year, and after completing two terms in that body, he was elected to Congress, where he was kept continuously for eight years. During his Congressional service he was engaged in the most important as well as exciting and interesting scenes which occurred in the capital, and during this period a warm and intimate friendship was formed between him and Mr. Webster, which survived until transmuted to veneration on the death of the latter.

In 1852 he was appointed by President Fillmore Minister to Brazil. Returning to his native country in 1854, he found that the anti-slavery movement had made extraordinary progress, and he at once espoused the principles of the Republican party, then in its infancy. In September, 1859, he addressed a large meeting in Dayton, and it is memorable that in his speech on that occasion he was first to propose Abraham Lincoln for the Presidency of the United States. In the course of his address he said : ·

" If the Republican party of this country—if the thinking, liberty loving men of this country want an honest—sensible man to lead them in the coming campaign, they cannot do better than nominate the distinguished gentleman from Illinois, Abraham Lincoln." In after years Mr. Lincoln frequently related this incident, and declared that Mr. Schenck was the first man who had in a public address named him for the Presidency. Subsequent to the Dayton speech, in the Chicago Convention, Mr. Schenck was largely instrumental in securing the nomination of Lincoln, and in the campaign which followed he took the stump at Mr. Lincoln's personal request.

The war came, and the veteran of many hotly contested political battles

CAMPAIGN OF 1852.

was among the first to offer his services to his country. He appeared at the capital before the echo of the fire on Fort Sumpter had died away, and tendered his services to the President. Mr. Lincoln said to him : " Schenck, can you fight?" " I don't know, sir, but I can try," was the characteristic reply. " And I am sure you will succeed," said the President ; " you have it in your blood, and I am going to give you a chance to try. You shall be made a brigadier-general."

How well General Schenck verified the President's predictions, the following letter illustrates :

" WAR DEPARTMENT, WASHINGTON CITY. September 18. 1862.

" MY DEAR SIR : No official act has been performed by me with more pleasure than the just tribute to your ability and patriotism by the enclosed appointment to the rank of major-general, for gallant and meritorious service to your country. It is my hope your health may soon permit you to accept a command befitting the rank. My regret for the painful suffering you now endure from the wound received on the field of battle is enhanced by the need the Government has at this moment for your service. With sincere regard, I am your friend,

" EDWIN M. STANTON.

" To MAJOR-GENERAL SCHENCK."

In December, 1863, General Schenck was again elected to Congress, when he resigned his commission in the army. He held a seat in the House of Representatives till his appointment, in 1870, by President Grant, to be United States Minister to England. At the Court of St. James he remained five years. Returning to America in 1876, he declined a renomination for Congress, and sought the repose which his feeble health demanded.

PRESIDENT PIERCE'S CABINET.

Secretary of State.—William L. Marcy, of New York, appointed March 7th, 1853.

Secretary of the Treasury.—James Guthrie, of Kentucky, appointed March 7th, 1853.

Secretary of War.—Jefferson Davis, of Mississippi, appointed March 7th, 1853.

Secretary of the Navy.—James C. Dobbin, of North Carolina, appointed March 7th, 1853.

Secretary of the Interior.—Robert McClelland, of Michigan, appointed March 6th, 1853.

Postmaster-General.—James Campbell, of Pennsylvania, appointed March 7th, 1853.

Attorney-General.—Caleb Cushing, of Massachusetts, appointed March 7th, 1853.

ROSCOE CONKLING.

CHAPTER XVIII.

CAMPAIGN OF 1856.

DEMOCRATIC NOMINEES.

For President.
JAMES BUCHANAN of Pennsylvania.

For Vice-President.
JOHN C. BRECKINRIDGE of Kentucky.

REPUBLICAN NOMINEES.

For President.
JOHN C. FREMONT of California.

For Vice-President.
WILLIAM L. DAYTON of New Jersey.

AMERICAN OR KNOW-NOTHING NOMINEES.

For President.
MILLARD FILLMORE of New York.

For Vice-President.
ANDREW J. DONELSON of Tennessee.

CONVENTIONS AND NOMINATIONS.

THE Democratic National Convention, at Cincinnati, June 2d, nominated James Buchanan and John C. Breckinridge.

The Republican party, at its first national convention, held at Philadelphia on the 17th of June, 1856, nominated John C. Fremont and William L. Dayton.

The American or Know-Nothing party met in national convention at Philadelphia February 22d, 1856, and nominated Millard Fillmore and Andrew J. Donelson. The dissatisfied minority rejected the platform adopted at this convention, and under the name of North Americans held a convention at New York on the 12th of June following, and nominated Nathaniel P. Banks, of Massachusetts, and W. F. Johnson, of Pennsylvania.

The remnant of Whigs and the Silver Grays met in national convention at Baltimore on the 17th of September, and indorsed the American nominees.

The electoral count following this election gave Buchanan 174 votes, General Fremont, 114, and Millard Fillmore, 8.

ABRAHAM LINCOLN.

In a humble cabin, standing on a knoll near the south fork of Nolin Creek, Kentucky, Abraham Lincoln, the son of poor and uneducated parents, was born on February 12th, 1809. When only eight years of age he was taken by his parents to a new home in what is now Spencer County, Indiana. There he grew up, in the midst of a wild region, with few educational advantages. He once wrote of himself, that on coming of age "somehow I could read, write, and cipher to the Rule of Three, but that was all." All that he afterward acquired he "picked up from time to time under the pressure of necessity."

Farm hand, rail-splitter, clerk in a country store, captain of volunteers in the Black Hawk War—all these things were his educators at a time of life when more favored young men are idling through the university. At twenty-three he returned to New Salem, Illinois, with considerable popularity among his neighbors by reason of his brief military career.

About this time he made his first speech in public before the New Salem Literary Society. Tall, awkward, with his hands thrust deep into his pockets, he stood before the little assemblage of his neighbors, who were already smiling in anticipation of one of the humorous stories for which, among his friends, he was famous. But he surprised them all with a keen and forcible argument, instead of flippant jokes. The State election was at hand, and admiring friends persuaded him to be a candidate for the Legislature. He made several short speeches on the stump in Sangamon County, in one of which he said : " My politics are short and sweet, like the old woman's dance. I am in favor of a national bank. I am in favor of the internal-improvement system and a high protective tariff. These are my sentiments and political principles." He was defeated, but received the whole vote of his precinct with three exceptions. But he had the satisfaction of being sent to the Legislature at the next and three succeeding triennial elections. This was the beginning of his public career. Thirty years more of active life remained to him, and in that time the crude stump-speaker of the Sangamon developed into the almost unequalled orator of Gettysburg.

In the campaign of 1844 Lincoln took a notable part, laboring for the success of his ideal statesman, Henry Clay. He engaged in joint debates, which excited popular feeling in Illinois and Indiana. The subsequent defeat of his candidate was a severe disappointment.

As the only Whig member from Illinois, Lincoln entered the Thirtieth Congress. After making his first speech he wrote to a friend : " I find speaking here and elsewhere about the same thing. I was about as badly scared, and no worse, as I am when I speak in court."

While gaining fame as a public man, Mr. Lincoln was earning his bread as a lawyer. His powers as a debater and speaker were not lost at the bar. Judge Drummond once said of him : " I have no hesitation in saying that he was one of the ablest lawyers I have ever known. If he was forcible before a jury, he was equally so with the court. . . . Let him be thoroughly aroused—let him feel that he was right, and that some principle was involved in his course—and he would come out with an earnestness of conviction, a power of argument, and a wealth of illustration that I have never seen surpassed."

One of the most remarkable campaigns in which Lincoln took part was in 1858, when he challenged and engaged Stephen A. Douglas in a series of joint debates in Illinois. All the political questions of the day were discussed, but especially slavery. Douglas was at that time one of the leading debaters in the United States Senate, whom the giants of that body had failed to discomfit. Lincoln's friends feared for him in the contest, but he held his own against the Little Giant. It has been said by a competent political observer : " Lincoln was candid, cool, truthful, logical, philosophical—never betrayed into an unfair statement. Douglas carried away the most popular applause, but Lincoln made the deeper and more lasting impression. These debates made Douglas Senator and Lincoln President."

His reputation as an orator spread throughout the country. In October, 1859, he was flattered by receiving an invitation to speak in New York City. He accepted, on condition that it might be a political speech, and set the date far ahead, in order that he might make thorough preparation. It is said that no effort of his life cost him so much labor as this one. In February, 1860, he went to New York to fulfil his engagement. He was surprised and embarrassed to find an immense audience assembled in Cooper Institute to hear him. The poet Bryant introduced him as "an eminent citizen of the West, hitherto known to you only by reputation." In low tones he began his great speech on the slavery question, and as he proceeded gained such confidence and became so eloquent that the next day the *Tribune* said : "The tones, the gestures, the kindling eye, and the mirth-provoking look defy the reporter's skill. No man ever before made such an impression on his first appeal to a New York audience."

As President, Lincoln made two speeches, which have won him his greatest fame as an orator—the short address delivered at the laying of the corner-stone of the soldiers' monument at Gettysburg, and his second inaugural, concluding with that eloquent sentence : "With malice toward none, with charity for all, with firmness in the right, as God gives us to see the right, let us finish the work we are in—to bind up the nation's wounds, to care for him who shall have borne the battle, and for his widow, and his orphans ; to do all which may achieve and cherish a just and a lasting peace among ourselves and with all nations."

A few weeks later the bullet of an assassin closed his eloquent lips forever, and the "nation's wounds" for a time gaped afresh.

STEPHEN A. DOUGLAS.

Stephen A. Douglas and Abraham Lincoln—rivals for the same woman's hand and heart, for a United States Senatorship, and for the Presidency, political foes for a generation, political friends at the last in the hour of their country's peril.

Douglas was a Vermont boy, the son of a physician, who left him fatherless when two months old; fifteen years he spent on a farm with his widowed mother, and then apprenticed himself to a cabinet-maker; hard work impaired his health, and, the opportunity offering, he spent several years in study. In 1833, when only twenty years of age, he set out for the West to finish his law studies, to support himself meanwhile, and lay the foundations for his great career. He reached Winchester, Illinois, with thirty-seven and a half cents in his pocket, acted as clerk to an auctioneer for a few days, opened a school, which was successful, pursued his law studies in the evenings, and within a year was admitted to practice. From that time his course was rapidly upward. Before he was twenty-two he was elected by the Legislature of Illinois Attorney-General of the State. Within a year he was elected to the Lower House of the Legislature, and was its youngest member; and in 1838, having just reached the required age of twenty-five, he ran for Congress on the Democratic ticket, and was only defeated by five votes. He, however, became a member of that body in 1843, and held the office until transferred to the Senate, in 1847. He was still a Senator at his death, in 1861.

As a campaign speaker in 1840, when Harrison and Van Buren were candidates for the Presidency, Douglas made a great impression. Isaac M. Arnold, an Illinois Congressman, once wrote of him: "He spoke always with great fluency and power. He seized the strong points of his case, and enforced them with great vigor. Quick and ready to seize the weak points of his antagonist, he would drive them home with strong and well-applied blows, never being disposed to yield an advantage which he had once obtained."

The Compromise measures of 1850 were supported by Mr. Douglas, and on returning to his home in Illinois he found his course vehemently assailed. On October 24th he made a great speech at Chicago in his own defence. In it he laid down the principle which, then and thereafter, guided him in the slavery agitation—that "every people ought to possess the right of framing and regulating their own internal concerns and domestic institutions in their own way. These things are all confided by the Constitution to each State to decide for itself, and I know of no reason why the same principle should not be extended to the territories."

During the campaign of 1852 Douglas and Lincoln, now leaders of rival parties, crossed swords in debate. Douglas took the stump for Pierce, speaking in twenty-eight States. His first speech was made at Richmond,

Virginia, and was scattered throughout the Union, but especially in his own State of Illinois. Lincoln felt called upon to answer it in a speech at Springfield. One of his biographers admits that "none of his public performances was more unworthy of its really noble author than this one." But these two were to meet later in no unequal contest.

One of the greatest debates in which Douglas ever took part was in the Senate, in 1854, when he introduced the Kansas-Nebraska bill, repealing the Missouri Compromise, and probably hastening the civil war by a generation. Douglas made the opening speech. He was his party's idol, and in his physical and intellectual prime, possessing all the qualities of a great popular leader. A writer on that contest says: "He brought to the accomplishment of his object, in the passage of his bill, his vast influence, his indomitable energy, and unyielding determination. His speech on the bill was able and eloquent, but bitter, defiant, and abusive." When he returned to Illinois, after the passage of the bill, he was greeted with a storm of indignation.

At the State fair in Springfield, a great crowd assembled to hear his defence. He was confident and arrogant, but spoke with all his great ability, to an unsympathetic audience. Lincoln was present, and on the following day replied in a great speech, which aroused the audience to boundless enthusiasm. Goaded by their cheers and his own discomfiture, Douglas sprang to the platform, asserting that he had been abused, but "in a perfectly courteous manner." He spoke several hours, but, it is said, without his usual success. Soon after, at Peoria, the two men met again in debate, and again did Lincoln carry the audience with him.

The great joint debate of Douglas and Lincoln, in 1858, has already been alluded to in the preceding sketch of Lincoln. "Great political parties," says one writer, "paused to watch its progress, and looked with eager solicitude upon every movement of the champions." The style of Douglas was "bold, defiant, aggressive, vigorous. He was fertile in resources, terrible in denunciation, familiar with political history . . . and unquestionably the most formidable man in the nation on the stump." The people were with Lincoln, as shown by the total vote in the State, but the Legislature returned Douglas to the Senate.

When, a few years later, both were candidates for the Presidency, the people of the country declared for Lincoln. The Union was threatened. Then Douglas threw aside his political prejudices for the sake of his country. He had an interview with President Lincoln, in which he assured him that he was fully prepared to sustain the Government and its head in the exercise of all constitutional functions to preserve the Union. At Springfield and Chicago he made speeches upholding the President. "There can be no neutrals in this war," he said, "only *patriots* or *traitors*."

A month later he was on his death-bed, and used his ebbing strength to dictate a letter urging patriotic men to sustain the Union, the Constitution, the Government, and the flag. On June 3d, 1861, he died, his last coherent utterances being a wish for his country's honor and the defeat of her enemies.

ANSON BURLINGAME.

Anson Burlingame was born in New Berlin, Chenango County, New York, on the 14th of November, 1820, and died in St. Petersburg, Russia, on the 23d of February, 1870. When Anson was three years old his father, who was a farmer, removed his family to Seneca County, Ohio, where they lived ten years, leaving in the year 1833 for a farm at Detroit, and again moving, two years later, to another farm at Branch, Michigan. In 1837 Anson entered the University of Michigan, and six years later went to Cambridge, Massachusetts, for the purpose of studying law at Harvard University, where he was graduated in the year 1846. He began the practice of the law in Boston, and a year or two later was well known as an active member and a popular orator of the Free-Soil party, which had just come into existence.

In the year 1848 he acquired a wide reputation as a public speaker, supporting Van Buren and Adams in the campaign of that year.

Massachusetts elected him to the Senate in 1852, and in 1853 he served as a member of the State Constitutional Convention, being elected by the town of Northborough, although he lived in Cambridge.

He joined the American party on its formation in 1854, and was in that year elected by it to the Thirty-fourth Congress. In the following year he co-operated in the formation of the Republican party, to which he steadily adhered, and was a most hearty supporter. In Congress he bore himself with courage and address, and was recognized as one of the ablest debaters on the anti-slavery side of the House. For the severe terms in which he denounced the assault committed upon the person of Senator Charles

Sumner by Preston S. Brooks, in 1856, he was challenged by Brooks. He promptly accepted the challenge, and named rifles as the weapons to be used, and Navy Island, just above Niagara Falls, as the place of fighting. To the latter proposition Mr. Brooks objected, alleging that, in order to meet his opponent in Canada, in the then excited state of public feeling, he would have to expose himself to popular violence in passing through "the enemy's country," as he called the Northern States. The manner in which Mr. Burlingame conducted himself greatly raised him in the estimation of his friends and of his party, although the matter presently fell through; and on his return to Boston at the end of his term, he was received with distinguished public honors. He was re-elected to the Thirty-fifth and Thirty-sixth Congresses; but failing, after an animated and close contest, to be returned to the Thirty-seventh, his legislative career ended in March, 1861. He was immediately appointed by President Lincoln Minister to Austria; but that government declining to receive in a diplomatic capacity a man who had spoken often and eloquently in favor of Hungarian independence, and had moved in Congress the recognition of Sardinia as a first-class power, Mr. Burlingame was then sent as ambassador to China. In 1865 he returned to the United States, intending to resign his office, but he was so strongly urged by the Secretary of State to resume his functions for the purpose of carrying forward important projects and negotiations which he had himself initiated, that he finally consented. When, in the year 1867, he announced his intention of returning home, the regent of the empire, Prince Kung, offered him the appointment of special ambassador to the United States and the great European powers for the purpose of framing treaties of amity with those nations—an honor never before conferred on a foreigner. This position Mr. Burlingame accepted. In the year 1868 he went to England, and from thence to France, Denmark, Sweden, Holland, and Prussia, and was most favorably received in all these countries. Reaching St. Petersburg early in the year 1870, he became a victim to pneumonia, dying after an illness of only a few days.

WADE HAMPTON.

WILLIAM H. SEWARD.

William H. Seward was born at Florida, Orange County, New York, on the 16th day of May, 1801. His father was a physician and merchant, who, after accumulating a moderate fortune, was appointed judge of one of the inferior courts.

At a very early age William exhibited a fondness for books, and committed a most unusual offence by running away from home to attend school. At the age of nine years he was sent to Farmer's Hall Academy, in Goshen, which had numbered among its pupils Noah Webster and Aaron Burr.

He made rapid progress in that institution, and in 1816 he entered Union College, from which he graduated with high honors, though six months of his senior year he spent in teaching in the State of Georgia.

After graduating he commenced the study of law in New York City, and completed his course with Ogden Hoffman and John Duer at Goshen, and was admitted to the bar in 1822. In the following year he removed to Auburn, and formed a partnership with Judge Miller, whose daughter he married in 1824.

As a lawyer he soon became distinguished for originality of thought, independence of action, and an industrious devotion to his profession that brought him a large practice and high reputation.

Mr. Seward's mind early led him to a consideration of political subjects. His father was a conspicuous Jeffersonian Republican, and his natural instincts, as well as his early education, led him to adopt the same political principles. In 1824 he was selected, by a Republican county convention, to prepare the address for the occasion, although scarcely old enough to vote. In several orations at this early period of his life the same fervent devotion to the cause of liberty was manifested which ever afterward marked his public career. In 1827 he appeared as the champion of the struggling Greeks, and by his youthful eloquence secured large contributions to the fund raised in this country for their defence. One of the largest political conventions that had ever assembled in the State of New York was held at Utica in 1828, composed of young men favorable to the election of John Quincy Adams to the Presidency. Mr. Seward presided over this convention with great ability. The same year he was offered a nomination for member of Congress, but declined the honor.

The anti-Masonic party was at this time rising into temporary and local importance, and Mr. Seward and his friends affiliated themselves with it, believing that it afforded the best position for a successful resistance to the national and State administrations which he opposed.

By this party Mr. Seward was elected a State Senator, in 1830, by a large majority, although his district had, the preceding year, given a large majority to the opposing party's candidate. Not yet thirty years old, he entered the Senate, and at the same time became, *ex-officio*, a judge in the highest court of the State, and the peer of men venerable in years and distinguished for talent and experience.

In 1834 Mr. Seward was nominated for Governor, but was defeated by William L. Marcy, although in every county he ran ahead of his ticket. Among the charges brought against him in this and the subsequent successful canvass was that of being "a young man." But a little over thirty, he had aspired to an office which had thus far only been held by the ablest and ripest statesmen in the State.

In 1838 he again ran for the office of Governor, and defeated his opponent, the distinguished Governor Marcy, by ten thousand majority. During the canvass he spoke in all sections of the State, and the revolution in politics which then occurred, and which assumed from the circumstances a national importance, was largely attributed to his exertions. He was re-elected Governor in 1840, but declined to be a candidate in 1842, and retired from the office on the 1st of January, 1843.

The administration of Governor Seward was, in many respects, the most remarkable of any in the history of the Empire State; and many wise and thoughtful statesmen regarded it as more influential in shaping the political issues which followed in the next twenty years, than any other event of that and subsequent periods. During his administration occurred the anti-rent difficulties; the enlargement of the Erie Canal, largely the result of his foresight and energetic advocacy; the eradication of the laws for imprisonment for debt, and every vestige of slavery from the statute books; the reformation of the penitentiary system, and those reforms in the severity of criminal sentences which betokened the dawning of an era of greater humanity; the promotion of the agricultural interests of the State; the creation and fostering of normal schools, and the extension of the privileges of the public schools to all classes. But pre-eminently was his administration known for its action relative to slavery. In 1844 Mr. Seward made political addresses in all sections of the State for Mr. Clay, though he did not favor his nomination. The greater part of Mr. Seward's time after leaving the executive chair of the State, to 1849, was devoted to his profession, and it was during this period that he acquired his great fame as a lawyer and took part in some of the most notable cases in judicial annals. Among them may be mentioned the case of James Fenimore Cooper against Horace Greeley for libel in the *Tribune*, in which he appeared for the defendant. The case of William Freeman, indicted for the murder of the Van Nest family, in which he appeared for the accused, resulted in a verdict of insanity.

In 1848 he warmly supported the election of General Taylor, and declaimed through the canvass with unusual energy. It was during that campaign, though not the first time, that he announced his idea, since so widely known and so often discussed, of "the antagonistical elements of society in America—Freedom and Slavery"—and which was subsequently formulated by him into that pithy expression, "the irrepressible conflict."

In 1849 Mr. Seward was elected to the United States Senate. He was the friend of General Taylor, and that President extended to him full confidence. The nomination of General Scott, in 1852, met Mr. Seward's hearty approval, and again he advocated throughout his State and in other sections of the Union the principles of the Whig party and the election of its candidates. Notwithstanding the election resulted in the overwhelming defeat of the Whigs, Mr. Seward, undismayed by the disaster, resumed his place in the Senate with his characteristic calmness and assiduity. In February, 1855, Mr. Seward was re-elected to the Senate by a large majority, against the determined opposition of both the American and Democratic parties. The nomination of General Fremont for the Presidency by the Republican party in 1856 was a serious disappointment to many of Mr. Seward's friends; but he manifested no disappointment, and entered upon the canvass with great zeal and energy. The Republicans were defeated, but not demoralized, and under Mr. Seward's leadership in the Senate they gained strength and influence for the more desperate conflict soon to follow.

Early in 1860 it seemed likely that the Republican party—strong and united—would reward the great and able statesman for his years of devotion to the principles of which it was an embodiment, to a nomination for the Presidency; and while in the Chicago Convention of that year he was the leading candidate, yet other considerations were thought to justify, and even render imperative, the nomination of Abraham Lincoln, and Mr. Seward gracefully yielded what proved his last opportunity of becoming the nominee for that high office.

In 1861 he was called into Mr. Lincoln's Cabinet as Secretary of State, in which he conducted the delicate and arduous duties connected with foreign affairs, during the whole of the civil war, with marked industry, sagacity, and success.

The war of secession had been begun for the purpose of establishing an empire, of which the corner-stone was to be slavery—an empire built of the ruins of the Republic. Upon this great and exciting topic and its just solution Mr. Lincoln and Mr. Seward were united, and it was fortunate for the President and the country that such an able prime-minister was at the head of the Cabinet.

In the spring of 1865 Mr. Seward was thrown from his carriage, and while lying in his bed in a crippled state, on the 14th of April, 1865, the assassin Paine entered his room, dangerously wounded his son, and with a poniard inflicted wounds upon him, which were at first believed to be fatal, but from which he slowly recovered.

He continued in office under Andrew Johnson, when he conducted the negotiations by which the United States purchased from Russia those territories in North America which are now called Alaska. In dissonance with nearly the whole of the Republican party he sustained President Johnson in his opposition to the reorganization measures adopted by Congress.

Late in the summer of 1870, notwithstanding his feeble health, he began a tour around the world, visiting Southern Europe, Turkey, Palestine, Egypt, India, China, and Japan. He was everywhere received with demonstrations of profound respect throughout his journey, and after his return home he superintended the preparation of a work descriptive of his travels. The venerable statesman died at his home in Auburn on the 10th of October, 1872.

PRESIDENT BUCHANAN'S CABINET.

Secretaries of State. —Lewis Cass, of Michigan, appointed March 6th, 1857; Jeremiah S. Black, of Pennsylvania, appointed December 17th, 1860.

Secretaries of the Treasury.—Howell Cobb, of Georgia, appointed

CAMPAIGN OF 1856.

March 6th, 1857; Philip F. Thomas, of Maryland, appointed December 12th, 1860; John A. Dix, of New York, appointed January 11th, 1861.

Secretaries of War.—John B. Floyd, of Virginia, appointed March 5th, 1857; Joseph Holt, of Kentucky, appointed December 31st, 1861.

Secretary of the Navy.—Isaac Toucey, of Connecticut, appointed March 6th, 1857.

Secretary of the Interior.—Jacob Thompson, of Mississippi, appointed March 5th, 1857.

Postmasters-Generals.—Aaron V. Brown, of Tennessee, appointed March 6th, 1857; Joseph Holt, of Kentucky, appointed March 14th, 1859; Horatio King, of Maine, appointed February 12th, 1861.

Attorneys-General.—Jeremiah S. Black, of Pennsylvania, appointed March 5th, 1857; Edwin M. Stanton, of Ohio, appointed December 31st, 1860.

CHAPTER XIX.

CAMPAIGN OF 1860.

REPUBLICAN NOMINEES.

For President.
ABRAHAM LINCOLN of Illinois.

For Vice-President.
HANNIBAL HAMLIN of Maine.

DEMOCRATIC NOMINEES.

For President.
JOHN C. BRECKINRIDGE of Kentucky.

For Vice-President.
JOSEPH LANE of Oregon.

DEMOCRATIC NOMINEES.

For President.
STEPHEN A. DOUGLAS of Illinois.

For Vice-President.
HERSCHEL V. JOHNSON of Georgia.

CONSTITUTIONAL UNION NOMINEES.

For President.
JOHN BELL of Tennessee.

For Vice-President.
EDWARD EVERETT of Massachusetts.

CONVENTIONS AND NOMINATIONS.

The Democratic National Convention met at Charleston, South Carolina, on the 23d of April, 1860. Party history records few more memorable events. All the States were represented. A majority and two minority reports were presented by the committee on resolutions. The convention adopted the principal minority report, whereupon the delegations from Alabama, Florida, Mississippi, Texas, and portions from Arkansas, Louisiana, North and South Carolina withdrew from the convention. Balloting for candidates then began, but after fifty-seven had been cast without a selection, the convention adjourned to meet in Baltimore on the 18th of June. The withdrawing delegates decided to meet in Richmond on the 11th of June.

At Baltimore it was found there were contesting delegations from several States. The subject was referred to the committee on credentials, which made three reports. The convention adopted the majority report, when the Charleston scene was re-enacted, and the entire delegations of California, Delaware, North Carolina, Tennessee, and Virginia, and parts of Kentucky, Maryland, and Massachusetts withdrew. Stephen A. Douglas and Herschel V. Johnson were then given the nominations for President and Vice-President. The delegates who withdrew from this convention met at the Maryland Institute, in Baltimore, on the 28th of June, and nominated John C. Breckinridge and Joseph Lane.

A "Constitutional Union" convention from twenty States met at Baltimore, May 9th, 1860, and nominated John Bell and Edward Everett for the Presidency and Vice-Presidency.

The Republican National Convention assembled at Chicago on the 16th of May, delegates being present from all the free States, and from Delaware, Maryland, Virginia, Kentucky, and Missouri. Abraham Lincoln was nominated for the Presidency on the third ballot, receiving 354 out of 466 votes; his principal competitors being William H. Seward, Salmon P. Chase, and Edward Bates.

The November election gave Lincoln 180 electoral votes; Breckinridge, 72; Douglas, 12, and John Bell, 39.

GEORGE WILLIAM CURTIS.

It is a mooted question whether peculiar eras in the world's history produce and develop men having the special character, traits, and genius needed for the times, or are themselves produced by men who stamp their individualities upon the generations in which they live. Whether one or the other or neither of these theories be correct, it will not be denied that few eras have been better calculated to waken the latent eloquence of a people and produce a generation of orators of the loftiest type than that which brought the Republican party into existence. The breath of life was breathed into its nostrils by a theme, an issue, a purpose as grand and inspiring as ever agitated a race, shook a nation to its foundations, or nerved men to battle with all their might for a sublime abstract principle. The voices that attacked the institution of slavery and waged upon it a relentless warfare till its chains were broken and four millions of men had been lifted from bondage into freedom, were inspired by that depth and earnestness of feeling which is the sole source of all true eloquence. The generation that compassed the destruction of slavery in the United States was fertile in men made eloquent by the times and the theme, and not a few of them have left specimens of oratory which the world will not allow to be forgotten, but which will be cherished among the English classics so long as that tongue continues to be spoken or read.

Of the orators who bore a conspicuous part in the first Presidential campaign of the Republican party few are left to do battle still; but of those few, one of the most accomplished, steadfast, efficient, and popular is George William Curtis. Coming upon the political stage with all the enthusiasm, earnestness, daring, and attractions of youth in the Buchanan and Fremont campaign in 1856, he has borne a conspicuous and influential part in every campaign since, and has wielded a potent voice in the councils of the Republican party from its birth to the present time.

Mr. Curtis was born in Providence, Rhode Island, February 24th, 1824, though a direct descendant from one of the first settlers of Worcester, Massachusetts, from which place his father moved to Providence. His mother was the daughter of James Burrill, who was elected Attorney-General of Rhode Island in 1797, at the age of twenty-five, held that office for fifteen years, then became Chief Justice of the State, from which office, after

BENJAMIN F. BUTLER.

about one year's service, he passed to that of United States Senator, in which he died at Washington, in 1820, at the age of forty-eight.

Mr. Curtis's school days were passed chiefly in a boarding-school at Jamaica Plain, Massachusetts, and under a private tutor in New York, to which city his father moved in 1839. It being his father's design that he should lead a mercantile career, he was placed in a German importing house in New York at the age of fifteen. But the life and occupation that the mercantile house held out to him did not absorb his ambition or interest. He devoted much time to reading and thinking about what he read, and found in this the mistress whom he served with most heart and interest. In thus following the bent of his own mind, he became interested in the Brook Farm socialistic experiment at West Roxbury, Massachusetts. This was an association of idealists or transcendentalists, started by a score or so of men and women, many of whom have left their "footprints on the sands of time" by pursuits which they followed after that short-lived experiment was abandoned. The aim was a reorganization of society upon theories differing somewhat from Fourierism, though differing but little from it in its practical working and social life. Hawthorne's "Blithedale Romance," though not a description of the society, was founded upon or suggested by his experience as a member of the Brook Farm phalanstery, where he met the lady who became his wife. Mr. Curtis, with an elder brother, joined this society in 1842, and remained a year and a half, studying and working on the farm until the experiment was abandoned. The two brothers then went to Concord, Massachusetts, and lived with a farmer about two years, continuing to work in the field and study. Here Mr. Curtis became the intimate acquaintance and associate of the men whose names have made the historic town of the Revolution famous as the head-centre of transcendentalism in later times—Emerson, Hawthorne, Thoreau, and others. Here the desire of seeing the old world came upon him, and in August, 1846, he sailed for Marseilles, and spent a year travelling about Italy, visiting and studying the points of chief interest, and mingling much with American artists. About another year was spent in a similar way in Switzerland and Germany. Spending the third season in Egypt and the fourth in Syria and the East, he returned by way of England, where he spent a part of the summer, and arrived home in August, 1850, after an absence of just four years.

The years of preparation for the battle of life were now ended, and the time for beginning to act his part as a man had arrived. During his travels he had written letters for the New York *Courier and Inquirer* and also for the *Tribune*. Shortly after his return he published his first book— "Nile Notes of a Howadji"—and then became one of the editorial staff of the *Tribune*, where he was once more a companion of Charles A. Dana and George Ripley, with whom he had shared the life and disappointment of Brook Farm. In this capacity he wrote a series of letters to the *Tribune* from the fashionable watering-places in the season of 1851, which were subsequently published as a volume under the title of "Lotus Eating," illustrated by the artist Kensett, whom he had met in Italy. His pen was now very prolific, for, in addition to newspaper and magazine work, the second book founded upon his travels abroad—"The Howadji in Syria"— was published in 1852.

In 1853 *Putnam's Monthly* began its life, and Mr. Curtis became one of its editors and a frequent contributor to its columns. Here first appeared the children of his brain known to the world in book form as "The Potiphar Papers," "Prue and I," and some of the chapters of "Homes of American Authors." The magazine not being a success financially, the ownership soon changed hands, and Mr. Curtis became a part owner, but took no share in the business or financial management. Under the new proprietorship the financial affairs of the magazine went from bad to worse, and in 1857 the firm failed, with liabilities exceeding assets to such an amount that many long and laborious years of Mr. Curtis's life were devoted to liquidating his share of the indebtedness; but he continued until the last cent was paid, though, had his sense of honor permitted him to do as many who now rank high in the financial and social world of New York have done, he could easily have relieved himself of the obligation without payment. In 1857 he began writing the "Easy Chair" of *Harper's Monthly* and "The Lounger" of *Harper's Weekly*, and has since been permanently connected with the latter paper, passing from the subordinate position to that of its principal editor in December, 1863. It is by his work in this last position, extending over a period of more than twenty years, and covering one of the most critical periods in the history of the country, that Mr. Curtis has exerted his greatest influence upon public opinion and political action. During this period journalism has made its grandest strides to the rank of a profession, and wrested the shaping of public sentiment upon all questions from political and pulpit orators, and lodged it in the editorial rooms of the great journals. In this work no man in the United States has had a greater or more creditable influence than Mr. Curtis, as the audience of scores of thousands whom he has addressed weekly, for more than twenty years, through the columns of the journal which takes its tone from him, are well aware.

The general editorial management and writing of such a journal as *Harper's Weekly* would be sufficiently arduous duty for most men, and a sufficiently severe tax upon most busy brains ; but Mr. Curtis has found time for an immense amount of work beside. When the lyceum lecture system came into vogue, and became such a potent vehicle for instructing, rousing, and educating the people, Mr. Curtis entered the lecture field, and has been one of the most frequent and popular lecturers from 1853 to the present time. He has also delivered many addresses before college and literary societies and upon other public occasions. Upon the establishment of *Harper's Bazar*, in 1867, he began contributing to it articles under the title of " Manners upon the Road," which were continued about six years.

Mr. Curtis was an original and radical Republican. From his first appearance as a lyceum lecturer slavery and its abolition was a subject frequently discussed and earnestly advocated by him. He took the stump for Fremont in 1856, speaking in Pennsylvania, New Jersey, New York, and New England, and he has spoken more or less in every campaign since, and has taken an active part in politics at his home at West New Brighton, on Staten Island. He was a delegate to the national conventions which nominated Lincoln in 1860 and 1864, and bore a conspicuous part at a critical point of the proceedings in 1860. The venerable, fiery, and influential Joshua R. Giddings had become deeply offended at the rejections of the words " life, liberty, and pursuit of happiness," proposed by him as a part of the first resolution, and was upon the point of withdrawing from the convention in disgust and anger when Mr. Curtis, by great tact and an eloquent speech, which gave him great reputation, induced the convention to reconsider its action and adopt the resolution in a form that satisfied Mr. Giddings. He was also a delegate to the convention that nominated Blaine and Logan in 1884. He opposed both these nominations with all his might and influence, but remained in the convention to the end, and took part in all its proceedings. After the convention he refused to support the ticket, and carried his opposition so far as to advocate and use all his influence and that of the journal of which he is editor to secure the election of Cleveland and Hendricks, the candidates of the Democratic party.

Mr. Curtis is one of the men who has been prominent in politics without holding political office. He once ran for Congress as a matter of form in the hopelessly Democratic district in which he lives, knowing that he could not be elected. He was offered the office of consul-general to Egypt by President Lincoln in 1862, but declined it. He was offered the post of Minister to England and subsequently that of Minister to Germany by President Hayes, but declined. On the death of Henry J. Raymond, in 1869, Mr. Curtis was invited to accept the position of editor-in-chief of the New York *Times*, but declined. Having been one of the leading advocates of civil service reform, he was appointed by President Grant in 1871 a commissioner to draft rules for regulating the civil service, and was chosen chairman of the commission; but after serving a little over a year he resigned, on account of radical difference of views between him and the President on the subject of civil service reform. He was a member of the Constitutional Convention of New York in 1867 and a Presidential elector in 1868.

In person Mr. Curtis is about medium size, and has a strikingly refined and intellectual face. As a speaker his manner is very polished and graceful. He never rants or splurges. Though he can indulge in witticism and pleasant banterings on the stump, his addresses are always in the style of a finished essay or editorial. He is not an orator of impulse, who trusts to the inspiration of the moment or an audience to put words into his mouth. He is not a speaker to rouse the enthusiasm of masses or those whose political convictions are not based upon their reasoning and intelligence. His rare gifts as an orator would be substantially lost upon any but an intelligent and thinking audience; but given this he is one of America's most admirable speakers, his manner in speaking somewhat resembling that of the late Wendell Phillips, one of the most perfect orators that spoke the English tongue, the oration at the ceremonies in commemoration of whose life was fitly delivered by Mr. Curtis.

HORATIO SEYMOUR.

Horatio Seymour was born in Onondaga County, New York, in the year 1811. He received a thorough and liberal education in the best schools of the State. No pains were spared by his parents to fit him for taking a prominent position in public affairs, to which career he seems to have been devoted from his childhood.

Young Seymour in early life decided to adopt the law as his profession, and so industriously and vigorously had he pursued his studies that he was admitted to the bar when only a little more than twenty years old.

In his earlier years he took very little active interest in political affairs, but that rare, comprehensive, statesmanly ability which he possessed was called for in the councils of the State, and in the fall of 1842 he consented to the election of a seat in the Legislature. As was to be expected, Mr. Seymour took a commanding position in that body. He began the session with a local reputation, but when it closed he had made himself known and honored throughout the State.

In 1852 Mr. Seymour was elected Governor of New York, and was defeated for re-election in 1854. After this defeat Mr. Seymour returned to his home in the city of Utica. His high qualities of mind and heart had drawn to him at the outset of his political career a band of devoted friends and admirers, and every year increased their numbers, until at length he came to be regarded as the foremost man of the Democratic party in his own State, and one of the purest and most gifted leaders of that party in the Union. His views were eagerly sought on all the great questions of the day, and his utterances received the respectful consideration of all parties.

In the convention held at Charleston in 1860, when it became evident that the contest between the friends of Douglas and those of Breckinridge could not be settled amicably, Mr. Seymour's name was presented by the Southern delegates, with the hope that the two wings of the party would unite upon him as a compromise ; but Mr. Seymour would not consent to the use of his name at that time.

During the campaign of 1860 Mr. Seymour supported the regular Democratic ticket, and when the Secession movement began at once exerted himself to procure a peaceful settlement of the difficulty. He believed, with the great orator and statesman, Burke, that there never yet was a revolution that might not have been prevented by a compromise opportunely and graciously made, and urged the adoption of measures of conciliation and peace ; but the *extremists* of the North and South prevailed in bringing on the war, and the labors of the conservative men of the country in both parties were defeated. Mr. Seymour was again elected governor in 1863, and no State executive excelled him in patriotic loyalty to the Union.

Mr. Lincoln said, in acknowledgment of his services, that " no governor had done more to strengthen the United States Government in its hour of need than Governor Seymour."

Mr. Seymour is a copious and eloquent speaker, and his voice has been heard with telling effect in every campaign since 1840. He unites the closest reasoning with graceful oratory, and his earnest, candid delivery is but the echo of his honest convictions.

GALUSHA A. GROW.

Galusha A. Grow was born in Eastford, Connecticut, in 1824. His parents were very poor. When he was eight years old his father died, leaving six children, of whom Galusha was the youngest son. Mrs. Grow placed three of the children in the care of relatives, and taking with her the eldest son, the youngest daughter, and Galusha, then ten years old, removed from the hamlet of Voluntown, Connecticut, to a little farm in Lenox, in north-eastern Pennsylvania. Her chattels consisted of a yoke of oxen and one cow. Galusha drove the oxen for ploughing. The first year's crop consisted of a field of oats and a few acres of maize, and even that, it seemed at one time, would be taken from them. Pigeons in countless numbers flocked together and roosted in the neighborhood of the Grow farm. They were very partial to oats and corn, and farmers had to guard their acres carefully. Galusha was sent to keep the pigeons away. Taking his dinner in a basket to the field, a mile distant from the house, he perched on the ridge-pole of the barn, on the outskirts of the field, and with two long poles whacked on the shingles resounding blows whenever he saw pigeons flying over him to alight. So he spent the days until the corn and oats were too large for the pigeons to disturb. It was not until Galusha was nearly fourteen years old that he had an opportunity to attend district school regularly. Eager to learn, he was one among a few kindred spirits to form a debating society. The only time he had to prepare for the debates was by reading while at his daily tasks on the farm. Thrown on his own resources, the boy shipped as a hand on a lumber raft from Tunkhannock, on the Susquehanna River, to Marietta, a trip of five days. In a rough board cabin on the raft the men ate and slept. Galusha was cook as well as oarsman. Mrs. Grow established a little store at Glenwood Post-Office, near her old home, and Galusha, as her assistant, found more time for study. In 1838 he entered Franklin Academy at Hartford, Pennsylvania, and in 1840 he went to Amherst College. He won the reputation of a ready debater, and developed a gift for making a sound speech at short notice. His oration on graduating, in 1844, was on a political topic.

In 1844 Mr. Grow studied law in the office of the Hon. F. B. Streeter, at Montrose, and was admitted to the bar in Susquehanna County on April 19th, 1847. Study had undermined his health, and in the summer of 1850 he went into the dense hemlock forests of north-eastern Pennsylvania, and wielded the axe in peeling bark. The winter of that year he made surveys of land. Meanwhile Mr. Grow's abilities as a stump speaker began to be known. In the fall of 1850 the Hon. David Wilmot, Mr. Grow's partner, was the candidate of the Free-Soil branch of the Democratic party, and James Lowrey, candidate of the Pro-slavery branch of the party for Congress in the Twelfth Congressional District, withdrew, with the understanding that Mr. Grow, then almost unknown outside of the county in which he lived, should be supported by the Democrats. He was elected a week after his nomination, and in December, 1851, he took his seat in the Legislature at Washington. He was then twenty-seven years old, and the youngest member of Congress. Mr. Grow at once made his mark as an orator. With instinct that amounted to genius, he began agitation on a subject which afterward became, next to slave-holding, the most prominent question before the people's representatives. It was the question whether Government land, then beginning at Ohio and running westward over what is now the most productive part of the Union, should be taken up by actual settlers, or whether, on the other hand, corporations and capitalists should buy up and hold, for speculative purchases, those immense prairies. The question has long since been settled, and to Mr. Grow's eloquence and courage the country owes the decision of the question on the side of the people. His first speech in Congress was on that theme, and persistently in every Congress for ten years Congressman Grow advocated the measure. During the agitation of the slavery question Mr. Grow's voice was heard both in and out of Congress with no uncertain sound. He spoke in Pennsylvania cities, and his direct, clear, and vigorous reasoning went far to clear away every mist from the discussion. Horace Greeley said of him in 1859 : " Mr. Grow has exhibited fertility of resource, command of parliamentary tactics, a promptitude in seizing an opportunity, a wisdom in act, and a brevity of speech such as have been rarely exhibited in Congress." When Mr. Grow took his seat as Speaker of the House of Representatives on July 4th, 1861, his vigorous speech in behalf of the

Federal Government was applauded. Two years afterward, when his term of office expired, feeble health compelled him to seek rest and a change. A disease of the throat, from too frequent out-of-door speaking, had fastened itself upon him. He became a lumber dealer, and invested in oil. His health did not improve, and he spent the summer of 1871 on the Pacific coast, and in the fall of the year he went to Texas, where he remained as President of the Houston and Great Northern Railroad Company until 1875, when he returned to Pennsylvania, and with tongue and pen advocated the election of Governor Hartranft, the Republican candidate, who was elected. In the Presidential campaign of 1876 he spoke for Hayes not only in Pennsylvania, but also in Indiana, Ohio, and New York. He declined the mission to Russia tendered by President Hayes. Again, in 1880, Mr. Grow took the stump for Garfield in Pennsylvania, Ohio, and New York, which were the most critical States. His power as a speaker, it has been said, is founded in a strong moral sense and convictions, unselfish purposes, a patriotism which overrules all considerations of personal interest or partisan expediency, a vivid imagination, and that sympathy which is the requisite of every true orator. He is still in business, with his health improved, and has not ceased to speak for the welfare of the nation.

DANIEL DOUGHERTY.

Daniel Dougherty was born in the city of Philadelphia on October 15th, 1826. His father when a lad came to this country from Ireland. His mother was a native of Philadelphia, and his maternal grandfather was a volunteer in the War of 1812, and was killed at the battle of Lake Erie. Mr. Dougherty was educated in his native city, and was admitted to the bar on May 2d, 1849. From his early boyhood he evinced a taste for public speaking, and whether at home or wandering in the fields outside the city, whenever he could do so unobserved, he was declaiming. When a lad he was a prominent debater in several literary societies, and his rendition of the part of Marc Antony, in the play of *Julius Cæsar*, brought out by a thoroughly equipped Thespian association, is well-remembered by numbers of those who were in the crowded auditory. His oratorical talent had given him distinction in Philadelphia before his admission to the bar, and his first speech for the defence in the Smithers homicide case created a

STEWART L. WOODFORD.

marked impression. The judges, counsel on both sides, and the public press spoke in high terms of praise of the ability that he manifested as an advocate. Though the prisoner's guilt was evident, the jury, after remaining out six days and six nights, brought in a verdict of acquittal. This at once established the young lawyer's reputation, and laid the foundations for a career that has earned for Mr. Dougherty a large income from his practice and a wide reputation. At all times, whenever he appears in court in a case of any magnitude—and he has the good judgment never to attempt to make, before a jury, a great speech in an unimportant suit—the courtroom is crowded.

His address before the literary societies of Lafayette College in 1859, when he spoke upon the theme "Fears for the Future of the Republic," showed the stern independence of the man, pointing, as it did, in no uncertain language, to the indifference of the people to public affairs and the degradation and violence of party spirit. The address drew a picture which was considered at the time as far too gloomy and pessimistic, but which the awful realities of the war that soon followed stamped as bearing the impress almost of prophecy. This speech was quoted from at considerable length in the House of Commons by Bulwer Lytton before his elevation to the peerage. Some years ago, after many and urgent invitations, he was induced to prepare a lecture upon "Oratory." He delivered this lecture in all parts of the country, and the success that had attended this first venture in a rather unusual field encouraged him to write two other lectures, one upon "The Stage" and the other upon "American Politics." He received invitations from all sections of the United States, and during several seasons made frequent lecturing tours. He was, however, finally compelled to abandon the platform for the court-room, his professional practice demanding his undivided attention. As an evidence of Mr. Dougherty's popularity as a lecturer, it may be stated that he has netted over $20,000 from "Oratory."

His first political speech was made before he had reached his majority. It was delivered in the Pennsylvania gubernatorial campaign of 1847. The next year, in the Cass campaign of 1848, he "stumped" the northern range of counties in the Keystone State in company with Hon. Galusha A. Grow, they being young men of nearly the same age. Mr. Grow entered political life shortly afterward, and has since been Speaker of the House of Representatives of the United States. Mr. Dougherty clung to his profession, and has repeatedly declined political preferment. Though for many years a conspicuous political speaker, he has never aspired to be a politician, and has frequently publicly expressed himself as entertaining nothing but contempt for the tricks and trades of wire-pulle: and machine managers. He played a prominent part in the Pierce campaign in 1852. In 1856, while attending, as a spectator, the Democratic State Convention in Chambersburg, he was invited to address the convention, and his speech upon that occasion created intense enthusiasm, and became one of the features of that campaign. While Mr. Dougherty was speaking the venerable Josiah Randall, father of Hon. Samuel J. Randall, and a leader of the Whig party, but who had announced his determination to vote for Mr. Buchanan, entered the hall, and was invited to a seat among the delegates. The speaker, abandoning the line of thought, instantly addressed the venerable citizen, and advancing toward the latter extended his hand, and welcomed Mr. Randall to the faith and fold of the Democracy. This incident thrilled every auditor, and the dramatic scene was one long to be remembered. Nothing more striking shows the natural orator than his ability on the instant to rise with any emergency. This mental alertness forms an important part of Mr. Dougherty's success as an orator. It is illustrated in the above episode, as well as in an incident which occurred when he was making a speech on St. Patrick's day, in 1867, before the Friendly Sons of St. Patrick in New York City. The society then embraced a strong English element, and when, in replying to the toast of Ireland, the Philadelphia lawyer was picturing the political wrongs of that country, he was interrupted by the president, Judge John R. Brady, who said : " Sir, you are violating the rules of this organization, which do not allow any political allusions to be made."

Mr. Dougherty hesitated but an instant, and then, in his clear, ringing voice, and in his most impassioned manner, said : " Mr. President, overlook my enthusiasm, if you can, and, in the language of Edmund Burke, ' pardon something to the spirit of liberty.' " The reply had its instant effect, and the whole company rose from their seats, while cheer on cheer went ringing through the hall.

Mr. Dougherty opposed the Lecompton policy of President Buchanan, and became an ardent adherent of Mr. Douglas in 1860. Perhaps the most polished of his political speeches was one delivered in Philadelphia after the adjournment of the Charleston Convention and the reassembling of the same body in Baltimore. Although he had been a friend and admirer of Mr. Breckenridge, he bitterly opposed the election of that gentleman, believing that the Breckenridge movement meant nothing less than an attempt to dissolve the Union. He was unsparing in his denunciation of all its adherents, standing alone among the noted Democrats of Philadelphia for the straight-out Douglas ticket, which, without the help of politicians, and lacking the aid of the usual campaign methods, polled 9000 votes in Philadelphia !

After the election of Mr. Lincoln it became palpable that war was inevitable, and he wrote to Senator Douglas, entreating him to awaken patriotic enthusiasm by replying to the speeches of Senator Iverson, of Georgia, and others, who uttered, on the floor of the United States Senate, sentiments of treason against the Government. With the first signs of the coming war Mr. Dougherty broke from all partisan associations, and was among the foremost men of his city in furthering the Union cause. His voice could be heard everywhere preaching for liberty and union. And so he continued until the close of the war. Early in October, in the Lincoln campaign of 1864, his popularity was unbounded. At the announcement that he was to speak on behalf of Mr. Lincoln, Concert Hall was so crowded that even the president of the meeting was obliged to stand throughout, and thousands could not get near the hall. It was with the greatest difficulty that Mr. Dougherty himself could make his way to the platform. Two nights afterward, at Harrisburg, when the Hon. Horatio Seymour was to address a Democratic meeting and Mr. Dougherty was announced to speak at an Union meeting, the Philadelphia orator sent a polite note to the distinguished statesman from New York, inviting him to a joint discussion, the preliminaries to be at once arranged. Mr. Seymour, through the Hon. Hiester Clymer, politely declined the courteous challenge. Shortly afterward Mr. Dougherty was invited by the citizens of Boston, headed by Edward Everett, to speak for the Union cause in Faneuil Hall. Upon his appearance in that historic building he was received with enthusiasm. Upon his return to Philadelphia, after speaking in various places, among others in Cooper Institute, in New York, his reception in the Academy of Music in that city, where he was the only speaker, was perhaps the greatest ovation ever extended there to a private citizen. Though tickets had been issued, so dense was the throng that all the aisles and every available inch of room was filled, and it was found necessary to close the doors and to give positive directions that not another person should be admitted. With the close of the war Mr Dougherty devoted himself entirely to his profession, and for more than a decade of years never made a political speech.

During the Tilden campaign he addressed the Democracy of New York in Cooper Institute. Mr. Tilden honored him by personally requesting him to devote a portion of his time to addressing meetings in different parts of the Empire State, but he was compelled to decline by professional engagements. In his own city, however, he made a powerful speech in favor of the Democratic candidates.

In 1880, as the guest of the Americus Club of Philadelphia, he attended the National Convention in Cincinnati. Known as a friend of General Hancock and an advocate for his nomination, Mr. Dougherty was requested by R. Milton Spear, delegate at large from Pennsylvania, to take the latter's seat and present Hancock's name to the convention. The suggestion emanated from a number of the general's friends, who, late on the night before the nominations were to be made, extended, through Mr. Spear, the request to Mr. Dougherty. He accepted the proffered honor, and with little time intervening prepared the speech that, perhaps, more than anything else, tendered to make his name familiar in every part of the land. He evidently resolved to make it as brief as possible, epigrammatic, and with no unnecessary words. He plunged into his subject at once. His imposing presence at once riveted attention. His voice, clear as a trumpet, rang through the immense hall. His attitude and splendid declamation created the wildest enthusiasm, and when he had finished his five-minutes' speech the nomination was a foregone conclusion. It may be truthfully said that had General Hancock been elected, a single speech, occupying in its delivery only a few moments, had made a President of the United States.

During the campaign which ensued he bore a conspicuous part, speaking in all the battle States of the Union.

Mr. Dougherty's style of speaking varies with the occasion. When addressing the bench his manner is quiet and conversational, and frequently in important cases he writes out his argument. Speaking to the jury in important cases, or haranguing the people in mass, he is impassioned to the highest degree, and while not physically exhausted, he feels the strain for several days.

Daniel Dougherty is often seen at his best around the post-prandial board. He is a great social favorite. His character as a man stands unquestioned and his fellow-citizens of all political opinions bear witness to the integrity of his character and the purity of his motives.

PRESIDENT LINCOLN'S CABINET.

Secretary of State.—William H. Seward, of New York, appointed March 5th, 1861.

Secretaries of the Treasury.—Salmon P. Chase, of Ohio, appointed March 7th, 1861; William P. Fessenden, of Maine, appointed July 1st, 1864.

Secretaries of War.—Simon Cameron, of Pennsylvania, appointed March 4th, 1861; Edwin M. Stanton, of Ohio, appointed January 11th, 1862.

Secretary of the Navy.—Gideon Welles, of Connecticut, appointed March 5th, 1861.

Secretaries of the Interior.—Caleb B. Smith, of Indiana, appointed March 5th, 1861; John P. Usher, of Indiana, appointed January 8th, 1863.

Postmasters-General.—Montgomery Blair, of Maryland, appointed March 7th, 1861; William Denison, of Ohio, appointed October 1st, 1864.

Attorneys-General.—Edward Bates, of Missouri, appointed March 5th, 1861; James Speed, of Kentucky, appointed December 2d, 1864.

CHAPTER XX.

CAMPAIGN OF 1864.

REPUBLICAN NOMINEES.

For President.
ABRAHAM LINCOLN of Illinois.

For Vice-President.
ANDREW JOHNSON of Tennessee.

DEMOCRATIC NOMINEES.

For President.
GEORGE B. McCLELLAN of New Jersey.

For Vice-President.
GEORGE H. PENDLETON of Ohio.

CONVENTIONS AND NOMINATIONS.

THE Republican National Convention met at Baltimore on the 7th of June, when Abraham Lincoln was renominated for President and Andrew Johnson nominated for Vice-President.

The Democrats held their National Convention at Chicago on the 29th of August, and selected General George B. McClellan and George H. Pendleton for President and Vice-President.

WILLIAM M. EVARTS.

William Maxwell Evarts was born in Boston, Massachusetts, on the 6th of February, 1818. Whatever advantage may be reaped from hereditary gifts and educational advantages fell to his lot. His father was Jeremiah Evarts, Secretary of the American Board of Commissioners for Foreign Missions, who was graduated from Yale College in 1802, practised law in New Haven, edited the *Panoplist*, a religious monthly magazine, afterward the *Missionary Herald*, published in Boston, wrote many essays on the rights of Indians, and died in Charleston, South Carolina, in 1831, when William M. Evarts was thirteen years old. Grave and studious as a boy in the Latin school at Boston, he entered Yale College when fifteen years old, and was graduated in 1837, when he was nineteen years of age. In college he had already settled the direction of his life work, and although he was diligent in all his studies, yet logical and severe pursuits suited him best. Slender in frame, he had no aptitude for the rough sports of college boys, and wiseacres wagged their heads as they looked at his fine, intellectual face and feared for the brilliant young Evarts.

On completing the regular college course Mr. Evarts was nineteen years of age. At that time the Harvard Law School, with Justice Story and Professor Greenleaf in the faculty, was the most prominent institution of the kind in the country. Mr. Evarts finished the regular course in this institution, and in 1841 was admitted to the bar in New York City. In the metropolis his scholarly style as an orator, his thorough grounding in the principles of law, and intense application to details in his client's business soon made him conspicuous. Appointed Deputy United States District-Attorney in 1849, he held the position four years, and, besides discharging the general duties of the office in a way to deserve the respect of the Federal Government officers above him, and also the confidence of the people, he took part in the courts in many questions of national interest. Such questions were the prosecution of persons connected with filibustering expeditions to Cuba, the annexation of which to this country was a popular movement.

Later he was associated with President Arthur as counsel for the State in the celebrated Lemmon slave case, which they together carried from one court to another, and to final success. Two celebrated cases which Mr. Evarts has conducted successfully are the Parrish will case and that of the mother of President Tyler's widow, Mrs. Gardiner.

In the late war the building of rebel rams in England was a matter of great anxiety to the Federal Government. Mr. Evarts was sent twice to the British Government to represent the condition of affairs and the position of the United States in the matter, and through diplomacy and knowledge of international law succeeded in inducing the English authorities to action which checked the open building of rebel craft and reduced the advantages of the Confederate States in England in that respect to a minimum.

Mr. Evarts's connection with the impeachment proceedings of President Johnson, in the House of Representatives, in April and May, 1868, first brought him prominently before the whole country. He was principal counsel for President Andrew Johnson, and he obtained, by a majority of one vote, a refusal to sustain the articles of impeachment presented by the House of Representatives. It was a natural result of the trial that Mr. Evarts was appointed Attorney-General of the United States. He held the position from July, 1868, to March, 1869.

President Grant appointed Mr. Evarts counsel for the United States to present and defend the interests of the Government and the people before the Geneva Arbitration Committee to settle the amount of damage due the United States in the famous Alabama claims question. Opposed to the ablest legal minds in England, Mr. Evarts convinced the commission that England owed this country $15,000,000, and the sum was paid. In the suit brought against the Rev. Henry Ward Beecher by Theodore Tilton, in 1873, Mr. Evarts was Mr. Beecher's senior counsel.

In 1877 President Hayes appointed Mr. Evarts Secretary of State. His administration of the office was in every way creditable to the Government which chose him and to himself. Since 1881 a large law practice has employed his time. His residence is in a modest square brick house at Second Avenue and Fourteenth Street, detached from adjacent buildings and adorned with climbing ivy. He spends the summer months at his country-house, Runnemede, near Windsor, Vermont.

As an orator in politics, Mr. Evarts's relation to any political canvass, as he has himself described it, has been such as belongs to a private citizen who feels a share of interest and responsibility about public affairs. On the rostrum his manner is grave, dignified, and deliberate, as though he seeks to carry conviction by the unanswerable nature of his argument. A character-

CARL SCHURZ.

istic gesture is an impressive, sustained shaking of the fore-finger of his right hand in the air above his head when he approaches the climax of a long-continued argument. He is as fond of long sentences as is a German metaphysician. In reply to those who criticise his style of expression, he has said : "No one but criminals object to long sentences." Yet every phrase of his long sentences contributes to the evolving of the original conception in the speaker's mind, and phrase follows phrase until the sentence rolls to a majestic close. Mr. Evarts is the first chosen to speak on great public occasions—at the unveiling of the statue of a great man, at the placing of a corner-stone for an educational institution, at memorial celebrations, and, far from being of an ascetic temperament, his face is often seen at the banquet board. Around his after-dinner speeches plays a quiet humor, and to those who have sought to joke at his expense a sarcastic thrust of wit sets the tables in a roar.

Union and Yale College and Harvard University have conferred on him the degree of Doctor of Laws.

GEORGE H. WILLIAMS.

George H. Williams was born in Columbia County, New York, on the 26th of March, 1823. He was educated at the academy on Pompey Hill, in Onondaga County, where his father removed at an early day. He studied law with Hon. Daniel Gott, and at the age of twenty-one he was admitted to practise in the courts of that State. In the same year he immigrated to the then Territory of Iowa, and commenced the practice of his profession at Fort Madison. In 1847 he was elected Judge of the Fifth Judicial District of Iowa. He discharged the duties of that office for five years, when both political parties offered to join in his re-election, but he declined. In 1852 he was nominated by the Democratic State Convention of Iowa as one of the Presidential electors, and canvassed the State for Franklin Pierce. In March, 1853, chiefly upon the recommendation of Hon. Stephen A. Douglas, who was his personal friend, he was appointed Chief-Justice of the then Territory of Oregon, and immediately with his family removed there. He was reappointed Chief-Justice of the Territory by President Buchanan, but resigned, and resumed the practice of his profession in Portland. Many leaders of the Democratic party at the time the State government was formed were in favor of making Oregon a slave State, and that question, separate and apart from the Constitution, was submitted by the Constitution Convention to the people. Mr. Williams took decided ground against the establishment of slavery in the new State, speaking and writing against it, and the pro-slavery party was defeated, but his standing as a party man was greatly impaired by the contest. When the Secession movement was inaugurated Mr. Williams dissolved his connection with the Democratic party, and assisted in the formation of a Union party in his State. In September, 1864, he was elected by the Republican party to the United States Senate. Soon after the expiration of his Senatorial term he was appointed one of the Joint High Commission to settle by treaty with Great Britain the Alabama claims and other disputed questions between the two countries. His appointment was with special reference to the north-western boundary between the United States and Great Britain, which had been in controversy ever since the treaty of the 15th of June, 1846. In December, 1871, Mr. Williams was appointed Attorney-General of the United States.

Mr. Williams's voice has been heard in every Presidential campaign in all sections of his adopted State since 1856, and not infrequently in other States of the Union. He is a forcible, logical, and at times an eloquent speaker, always leaving with his auditors some impressive thoughts over which reasoning minds will ponder.

RICHARD B. HUBBARD.

Richard Bennett Hubbard is a native of Walton County, Georgia, and is now fifty-one years of age. His father, Richard Bennett Hubbard, Sr., was of Welsh ancestors, who, emigrating to America, bore a conspicuous part in the war of the Revolution, serving in Virginia and the Carolinas. His mother, Serena Carter, was a native of Georgia, and descended from the Carters and Battles, whose names are enfibred with the history of that State, distinguished as they were for patriotism, honor, and every manly virtue. His father died in the sixty-fifth year of his age, in Smith County, Texas, whither he had followed the fortunes of his only son. His aged mother still lives.

Mr. Hubbard's educational advantages have been of the best character, and he has well improved them. He is a graduate of Mercer University, Georgia, which institution he left at the age of eighteen, with honors. He subsequently passed through the law department of the University of Virginia, and graduated at the law school of Harvard University. In 1852 he moved to Texas and began the practice of his profession at Tyler, Smith County, where he has ever since resided.

His success was marked from the beginning. His superior talents, excellent attainments, tireless application, and strict fidelity speedily brought him into notice, and his persevering energy and eminent success at the bar placed him at the front, and early gave him a large and lucrative practice. Scarcely three years after his arrival in Texas he was not only recognized to be a sound lawyer and eloquent advocate, but also as a leader in politics.

In 1855 the Know-Nothing or American party had acquired great prominence, and threatened the overthrow of the then dominant Democracy. Democratic leaders saw that the newly-aroused prejudices of the people were about to give power to a proscription party, and that the very best talent of their party must be brought into requisition to disabuse the public mind. Henry A. Wise, then the most brilliant, powerful, and influential orator of Virginia, was put forward in his State to crush the rising power of the Know-Nothings. He did it after a long heated and intensely bitter campaign. What Henry A. Wise was to the Democracy of Virginia, Richard B. Hubbard was to the Democracy of Texas. He canvassed the State, aroused the sympathies of his party friends, and saved the State to the Democrats. It was during this campaign of 1855 that he gained the *sobriquet* of the " Eagle orator of Texas."

In the following year he again canvassed the State in the interest of his party. Early in the spring of 1856 he was chosen a delegate from Smith County to the State Democratic Convention, which met to choose eight delegates to the national convention to be held at Cincinnati. The State convention met at Austin, and Mr. Hubbard was chosen one of the eight delegates to Cincinnati, where he voted for Mr. Buchanan as the nominee for President of the United States. On his return home the party demanded of him still further services, and again the hustings of Texas rang with the powerful speeches of the gifted young orator. In 1859, when Mr. Buchanan was inaugurated President, Mr. Hubbard was appointed United States District-Attorney for the Western District of Texas.

This office he held but little over two years ; but during his official life he participated in numerous famous trials. In 1858 he resigned the office, and became a candidate to represent Smith County in the State Legislature.

Local considerations prompted this course. He had fulfilled his duty as an officer of the Federal court, and had won the confidence of the bench and bar, but the people of the State, and especially of Smith County, demanded his voice in their legislative council. His course in the Legislature to which he was elected was marked by prudence and ability, and his speeches in that body had much influence. He was an acknowledged leader of the Legislature.

In 1860 Mr. Hubbard was again chosen a delegate to the National Convention, which met at Charleston, South Carolina. In that convention he opposed the nomination of Stephen A. Douglas and advocated the selection of Breckinridge and Lane for President and Vice-President. The Republicans nominated Mr. Lincoln and the Americans Mr. Bell, of Tennessee. The election of Mr. Lincoln was followed by the Civil War, lasting from April, 1861, to April, 1865.

Mr. Hubbard raised the Twenty-second Texas Regiment of Infantry for the Confederate Army, of which he was made colonel. He was active during the war, his bearing throughout being that of a true patriot and soldier. As his fame in no degree rests upon his military record, it is only necessary to say that with him the war ceased when active hostilities were ended. He accepted, in good faith, the results of the war, forgot, as far as possible, the bitterness engendered by the conflict, everywhere counselled moderation and acquiescence in the inevitable, and went quietly to work to repair his shattered fortunes. His personal example exerted a healthful influence throughout the State. He did not resume the practice of law till some years later, and the disabilities imposed upon him by the Federal Government, in consequence of his connection with the Confederate Army, prevented him from taking an active part in political affairs.

During the period of reconstruction he devoted his energies to his private business, but was by no means a disinterested observer of passing events. Although he did not approve all the measures adopted by the general Government to restore the State of Texas to the Union, yet he was too wise and prudent to antagonize a power which he was impotent to control or even influence. He knew there was a time in the not distant future when the sons of Texas must resume control of the State machinery, and he patiently awaited the result. As soon as he deemed it prudent, he again began the practice of law, and soon found himself in the midst of professional business. This brought him prominently before the public again, and his friends insisted on his reappearance in the political field. In 1872 he was sent as a delegate to the Democratic State Convention to be held at Corsicana. He was then nominated as one of the electors for the State at large, and canvassed the State for Horace Greeley. Applause and welcome greeted him wherever he went, and although Mr. Greeley was not a favorite with the people of Texas, Colonel Hubbard was chosen elector by a majority of over 20,000.

In 1874 he was again sent as delegate to the Democratic State Convention which met at Austin. It was composed of about eight hundred delegates, and he was unanimously chosen its presiding officer and made chairman of the State Democratic Executive Committee. He was, by the action of his friends, a competitor for the nomination for the office of governor, and was the second choice of the convention, Judge Coke receiving the nomination. Colonel Hubbard was then, by a unanimous vote, nominated for lieutenant-governor, and was elected by a majority of over 50,000. The duties of this office he discharged with such distinguished ability as to win encomiums from every member of the Senate over which he presided; but the adoption of the new State Constitution vacated all the offices, and made a new election necessary. Colonel Hubbard was again unanimously nominated for lieutenant-governor, and was elected by a majority of over 100,000.

In December, 1876, Governor Coke was elected United States Senator, and Governor Hubbard assumed gubernatorial control of the State. No man ever became the chief executive of a great State under more auspicious circumstances, nor with a firmer purpose to render to the State and the people an essential and profitable service. Perfectly familiar with Texas, her resources, her needs, the inducements she offered to immigrants, and the necessity for extraordinary efforts to secure immigrants to till her soil and people her vast domain, he set to work intelligently to accomplish results of incalculable benefit to the State and to the South-west. His recommendations to the Legislature were accepted in the spirit in which they were offered, and the prominent measures of reform were adopted. The tide of immigration rolled over the State, from which there has not been and is not likely to be a refluent wave. Progress, like a spark falling on an inflammable mass, has spread throughout the vast territory, and the census of 1880 shows an immense increase in the wealth, population, and production of Texas. This grand consummation is in a large degree the result of Governor Hubbard's individual efforts.

Although Governor Hubbard had announced his intention to retire from active political life, the Democratic State Convention, held at Galveston in 1880, selected him as one of the delegates from the State at large to the National Convention that met at Cincinnati in June. His colleagues were distinguished citizens of Texas, and included some of her ablest men. The delegation was uninstructed, but it was probably known to every member of the State Convention that Governor Hubbard preferred General Winfield Scott Hancock to any other man as the standard bearer of the Democracy in the national contest. When nominations were made in the convention, and the name of General Hancock was presented, Governor Hubbard seconded the nomination in a speech of great power ; and this speech was supplemented by another made before a popular assembly on the evening previous to the final ballot. Both created great enthusiasm for General Hancock, who had endeared himself to the people of Texas by his patriotic course while commanding the Department of the South-west, and did much to secure his nomination. His speeches received universal praise for their eloquence and vigor, and were worthy of the man, of the Empire State of the New West, and of the great occasion, and were listened to by the representatives of more than half the people of the Union.

Governor Hubbard is the most popular orator in Texas. He is a social, genial gentleman, of high literary attainments and most pleasing address ; a fine specimen of the old type Southern orator, never speaking on public occasions without due preparation and moving the hearts and sympathies of those who hear him by feeling in his own bosom the emotions he arouses in others. His brilliant canvass of the State in 1872 as a candidate for elector and his impassioned oratory in 1873 awakened the Democratic party from the lethargy occasioned by the practical operation of the reconstruction acts of Congress, and aided largely in wrestling the State government from the hands of the Republican party. Perhaps there is no man more universally popular in Texas than Governor Hubbard. Though a private citizen, without office, and neither seeking nor desiring public station, yet he is everywhere received with marked honors by all the people, irrespective of party. This popularity is based not alone upon the fact that he is a magnetic speaker, but upon his worth as a citizen and his services as a man. He has given his talents and energies to advancing the interests of the State, developing its exhaustless resources, and bringing into it thousands of substantial citizens. He is a progressive man, and keeps pace with the age in which he lives. With broad, liberal, and comprehensive views of both State and national polity, he is not circumscribed by sectional lines. Devoted to the cause of the South in the late Civil War, he yielded to the arbitrament of the sword to which he appealed, and has forgotten the bitterness of the past. With true patriotism, he has devoted his talents, whenever opportunity offered, to the noble work of restoring fraternal good feeling among the people of our common country. In every position of public trust to which the people have called him, his performance of duty has been marked by strict fidelity and an earnest devotion to the public weal. He has honored every office held by him.

After retiring from the gubernatorial office in 1879, he devoted his time and talents to the development of Texas—by giving to her people *competitive* outlets for their trade. The organization of the Great Narrow Gauge System of South-western Railways was effected largely through him, and now reaches from Cairo, Illinois, 765 miles to Gatesville, Texas, 40 miles beyond the valley of the Brazos. His speeches before the solid men of St. Louis and their Merchants' Exchange aroused that people, and are remembered as masterpieces in moving capital to invest in independent competitive railways connecting the Great West with Texas and, through Mexico, to the Pacific coast.

In 1884 Governor Hubbard was elected a delegate at large to the Chicago Convention, and on the meeting of that body, on the 8th of July, Governor Hubbard was *unanimously elected* temporary chairman, which honor he acknowledged in a very effective speech.

Governor Hubbard is classed among the first of Southern orators, and his talents are not overestimated. He possesses personal magnetism in an eminent degree. His voice is full, sonorous, and powerful, never harsh or disagreeable. His manner is graceful, his diction chaste and elegant, abounding in appropriate tropes and similes, while his delivery heightens the effect of his speech. In argumentative discourse he is close, logical, and analytical, presenting his propositions with precision, yet never grows prolix or wearisome. In the persuasive art he excels, and never fails to arouse the sympathies of his hearers when sympathy is needed. As an advocate he has few equals at the bar, and on the rostrum he ranks with his ablest contemporaries. Behind all those natural gifts he enjoys rich culture and an industrious mind trained to regular labor, which has given him such eminent success as an executive officer.

There was no change made in President Lincoln's cabinet after his second inauguration, except that of Secretary of the Treasury. Hugh McCulloch, of Indiana, was appointed to succeed William P. Fessenden March 7th, 1865.

PRESIDENT JOHNSON'S CABINET.

April 15th, 1865—March 3d, 1869.

Secretary of State.—William H. Seward, of New York, continued.
Secretary of the Treasury.—Hugh McCulloch, of Indiana, continued.
Secretaries of War.—Edwin M. Stanton, of Ohio, continued ; John M. Schofield, of New York, appointed April 23d, 1868.
Secretary of the Navy.—Gideon Welles, of Connecticut, continued.
Secretaries of the Interior.—John P. Usher, of Indiana, continued ; James Harlan, of Iowa, appointed May 15th, 1865 ; Orville H. Browning, of Illinois, appointed September 1st, 1866.
Postmasters-General.—William Denison, of Ohio, continued ; Alexander W. Randall, appointed July 24th, 1866.
Attorneys-General.—William Speed, of Kentucky, continued ; Henry Stanberry, of Kentucky, appointed July 23d, 1866 ; William M. Evarts, of New York, appointed July 15th, 1868.

Albert Miller Card.

CHAPTER XXI.

CAMPAIGN OF 1868.

REPUBLICAN NOMINEES.

For President.

ULYSSES S. GRANT of Illinois.

For Vice-President.

SCHUYLER COLFAX of Indiana.

DEMOCRATIC NOMINEES.

For President.

HORATIO SEYMOUR of New York.

For Vice-President.

FRANCIS P. BLAIR, JR., of Missouri.

CONVENTIONS AND NOMINATIONS.

THE Republican National Convention met in Chicago on May 20th, and nominated General Ulysses S. Grant and Schuyler Colfax for the offices of President and Vice-President of the United States.

The Democrats met in national convention at the city of New York on the 4th of July, and nominated Horatio Seymour and Francis P. Blair.

HUGH JUDSON KILPATRICK.

In the beautiful valley of the "Clove," in Sussex County, New Jersey, on the 14th of January, 1836, was born the soldier and the orator, General Kilpatrick. He entered the military academy at West Point in his eighteenth year, and on the breaking out of the Rebellion he petitioned the President, with the signatures of the first class, for their immediate graduation, which was granted, and the young soldiers were at once sent to the field.

A volume would not encompass a recital of the invaluable services which Kilpatrick rendered his country in the dark days of its history, and to recount the deeds and heroic achievements of this valiant soldier would be to trespass beyond the limits of this work. After the close of the Rebellion General Kilpatrick was undecided in regard to his future calling. Although a thorough soldier, yet a soldier's life void of the exciting contests of the battle-field was an irksome one to him, and instead of an inactive soldier's life he resolved to abandon the army and pursue the vocations of peace. His widowed mother was living on the old homestead a few miles from Deckertown, New Jersey, and he concluded to resign his commission in the army, take up his residence from which he went a few years before a beardless boy, and become a farmer; but his restless nature would not be content with agricultural pursuits alone, and he was soon actively engaged in politics and espousing the Republican cause. During the Presidential campaign of 1864 and those which followed he became one of the celebrated speakers on the stump, and was universally recognized as inferior to none. He possessed a wonderful ability to electrify an audience, and was as enthusiastic and fearless on the rostrum in the field of politics as he had been in the saddle years before leading his brave soldiers in the "March to the Sea."

He spoke throughout the New England, Middle, and Western States, and was generally engaged in the State elections of very many of the Northern States. He was appointed United States Minister to Chili in 1866, and remained at his post until August, 1870.

On his arrival home he set about improving his farm, spending the summer there, and lecturing in the winter season. His first and most successful lecture was "Sherman's March to the Sea." Having borne a conspicuous part in the march he conceived the idea of embodying the events in a lecture ; and being possessed of a knowledge of the principal incidents connected with it, and peculiar power of description, particularly battle scenes, it at once became one of the most popular lectures of the day. It was first given in Music Hall, Boston, and was recognized by that city of acknowledged literature as a success. No other lecture in the country has been so often repeated.

He next prepared a lecture entitled "Incidents and Battle Scenes of the Rebellion." It was a compiled description of the various engagements, and was noted for its vivid description of the battle of Gettysburg.

General Kilpatrick was twice a candidate for the nomination of Governor of New Jersey. He was chairman of the New Jersey delegation which attended the Chicago Convention in 1880, and seconded the nomination of Chester A. Arthur for the Vice-Presidency. He was very earnest in presenting the claims of John Sherman for the Presidency, but finally voted for General Garfield.

During the campaign he spoke through the New England, Middle, and Western States, and was nominated for representative in Congress from his own district. It was Democratic by 5000 majority, but he was not a man to be daunted by that consideration. He had disregarded superior numbers during the war, and felt he could overcome majorities on the political field. He made a vigorous canvass, and was defeated, but he reduced the majority materially and made flattering gains in his own neighborhood and county. After the inauguration of General Garfield he was appointed to the Chilian Mission. He sailed from New York in June, 1881, for his post of duty.

Before leaving he complained of being very much reduced in strength, but attributed it to over-exertion, and expressed a belief that the trip and climate would improve his condition. Almost immediately on his arrival in Chili he began to complain of waning strength. In the hopes of improving his condition he was removed to a plantation a few miles from Santiago, but of no avail.

On the evening of December 2d, 1881, the grim rider whose shaft had been turned aside so oft on the battle-fields had won the victory, the strong arm lay motionless, and his bright eye was paled by death's cold touch.

In stature General Kilpatrick was five feet five inches in height, rather stout, and from habitual riding was inclined to stoop forward. He had a very prominent nose—which, it is said, Napoleon declared marked a great general—thin lips, and his gentle blue eye wore an expression of mildness, in direct contradiction to his record as a soldier; and in that capacity, which he so much exalted, he will live on the pages of his nation's history; and when centuries shall have sped and a grateful posterity shall turn the leaves, no name will inspire a higher admiration for valor or a deeper devotion to country than General Judson Kilpatrick.

CARTER H. HARRISON.

Carter H. Harrison was born in Fayette County, Kentucky, February 25th, 1825.

At fifteen he was sent to school to Dr. Lewis Marshall, brother of the chief-justice, and father of the celebrated Kentucky orator, Thomas F. Marshall. He was with him two years, and then went to Yale College, entering the sophomore class, and graduated in 1845. After graduating he returned home and studied law, but did not practise.

Having a fair competence, he went to Europe in 1851, and visited every part of England and Scotland, much of it on foot, for a closer study of the people and their characteristics. He travelled over the continent, Spain, Norway, and Russia excepted, passed into Egypt, and thence, with Bayard Taylor, did Syria and Asia Minor.

Taylor's " Land of the Saracen" was the result of their tour together. He returned to America in 1853. To complete his law studies he entered the Transylvania Law School at Lexington, and finished the course in 1855. In the same year he went to Chicago, and, foreseeing its future possibilities, decided to settle in that growing city. He there began the practice of law; but at that period, being inclined to diffidence, appearing before courts and juries was so averse to his tastes he relinquished the profession, and engaged in the real-estate business, which he found a more congenial vocation, promising a shorter way to fortune's goal.

It was not till 1870 that Mr. Harrison took any part in politics, or was known beyond the precincts of his city. In 1872 he was a Democratic nominee for Congress, but was defeated by a small majority.

In 1874, while abroad, he was again nominated for Congress and elected, and in 1876 he was re-elected. In 1878 he declined a renomination and in April, 1879, he was elected mayor of Chicago. In 1881 he was again a candidate for the mayoralty, and was re-elected by an increased majority, notwithstanding a strong press opposition. During these few years of Mr. Harrison's official life, he developed a readiness for speaking almost phenomenal, and is now regarded as one of the most brilliant orators of the West.

ROSCOE CONKLING.

One is not wise if, desirous of posthumous fame, he rests it upon popular or brilliant oratorical efforts. The wonder-working power of all oratory—that fascination which fades away as the person of the speaker vanishes—ploughs no deep furrow in the seed-field of time, but leaves behind only a pleasing tradition, more or less vague.

The dual essentials of a worthy public man—oratory and a capacity for work—are not often blended. But estimated on that basis, Roscoe Conkling is pre-eminently one of the leading orators of to-day, and in the national legislation of the past twenty years his mind and work are deeply impressed.

Roscoe Conkling was born at Albany, New York, October 30th, 1829. His father, Alfred Conkling, was a representative in the Seventeenth Congress, and was appointed by John Quincy Adams Judge of the United States for the Northern District of New York, in 1825, and Minister to Mexico, by Fillmore, in 1852. He was the author of several valuable books on law.

Roscoe received a common-school and academic education, and in Auburn and Geneva he studied law three years under his father's tuition, and in 1846 entered the law office of Spencer & Kernan, in Utica, New York. In 1848 he was appointed, by Hamilton Fish, District-Attorney for Oneida County, several months before he attained his majority. On the day he was twenty-one he was admitted to the bar, at which he had already acquired considerable reputation.

During the next decade he disclosed rare managing qualities, and was looked to as a leader in local politics. In law he ranked first as an advocate. The triumphs which he achieved at the bar, and which were his passport to public preferment, were gained before he reached the age of twenty-nine. He married Julia Seymour, a sister of Horatio Seymour.

In 1858 he was elected Mayor of Utica, and by a tie vote in the following campaign he was obliged to hold over for another year, as neither of the candidates qualified.

In November, 1858, he was sent to the Thirty-sixth Congress, and took his seat in December, 1859, a session noted for its long and bitter contest on the Speakership. He was re-elected in 1860, and entered the Thirty-seventh Congress at the opening of the special session convened by Lincoln, July 4th, 1861. In this Congress he was Chairman of Committee of District of Columbia, and also of a special committee to frame a bankrupt law. A candidate for re-election to the Thirty-eighth Congress, he was defeated by his old law partner, Francis Kernan, but at the election of 1864 he was successful, Mr. Kernan again being his opponent, and he resumed his seat in the Thirty-ninth Congress.

The fame of Mr. Conkling as an orator had preceded him, as had his reputation as a party manager. He startled the nation by a vigorous assault upon General McClellan, and gave the key-note for earnestness in all future war legislation at a time when hesitation and vacillation prevailed. In all monetary measures and legislation for the prosecution of the war, he was an active supporter.

In the fall of 1866 he was elected to the Fortieth Congress, but before that Congress met was chosen to succeed Judge Ira Carpenter as United States Senator from New York, and took his seat March 4th, 1867. He was re-elected in 1873, and again in 1879. He was a zealous supporter of General Grant's administration. The general policy of that administration toward the South was largely directed by Senator Conkling, who advocated it with all the power of his eloquence and all the potency of his personal and political influence. He was largely instrumental in the inception and passage of the Civil Rights bill.

One of the most important acts of Senator Conkling's political career was the part he took in framing an act for an Electoral Commission in 1876. In regard to the powers conferred upon the commission, he said : " Mr. President, I had supposed that the Constitution had raised not only a hedge and a fence, but a wall of limit to the powers it confers. I had supposed that when five of the most largely instructed and trusted members of the Senate, and five of the most largely instructed and trusted members of the House, were authorized to meet five judges of the highest and most largely instructed judicial tribunal of the land, we might trust to them to see what a court of Oyer and Terminer settles whenever it is called upon to determine whether it has jurisdiction to try an indictment for homicide or not. I had supposed that, giving it the instrument by which its jurisdiction is to be measured, we could trust this provisional tribunal of selected men to run a boundary and fix the line marking their jurisdiction."

Mr. Conkling attended the Republican National Convention in 1880, and was the leader of the famous 306. His speech in nominating Grant was a marvel of brilliancy, and his celebrated couplet will never be forgotten. He said :

> "And if you ask me whence he comes,
> Or what his name may be,
> He hails from Appomattox,
> And its famous apple tree."

The effect was electrical, and General Grant's nomination was only prevented by quick and judicious work. Mr. Conkling's speeches during this campaign were of the greatest help to the success of the Republican party.

His resignation as Senator soon after Mr. Garfield's inauguration is well-known recent history. This action caused great excitement through the country. Mr. Conkling was not re-elected, and he removed to New York City and devoted himself once more to the practice of law. He has met with success, and is building up a competency which political life never afforded him.

In his public speeches his power of repartee and faculty of gauging and carrying his hearers with him is unsurpassed.

During the campaign of 1880, in one of his speeches delivered in Western New York, Mr. Conkling, after an eloquent eulogy of his party, said : " And they say there should be a change. A change ! What for ? Will some kind Democratic friend in this audience tell me what benefit will come of a change ?" An excited but courageous Democrat cried out, " It will do away with the aristocracy of America." Conkling paused, and begged for a repetition of the words. Again the answer came, " It will do away with the aristocracy of America." " Do away with the aristocracy of America ?" said the orator. " Merciful heavens ! If there is an aristocrat in this audience, will he please hold up his right hand ?"

In 1858, as candidate for mayor, the workingmen were opposed to him for his alleged non sympathy. This opposition was cleverly manipulated by Mr. Conkling's political opponents, until it resulted in a published call for a *Workingmen's Meeting*, to nominate one more in unison with them. Mr. Conkling attended, and after listening to several speeches in which he was attacked, rose and said : " I attend this meeting *pursuant to call.* I am a working man, and earn my bread by the sweat of my brow. It does not seem to me that it makes any difference whether this perspiration is on the outside or the inside of my head." The opposition suddenly ceased.

Unthinking people are governed by prejudices. Little things sway them. A peculiarity of speech, a difference in dress, or a profusion or a scarcity of hair irritates them. No man in American politics has been more persistently misunderstood or malignantly misrepresented than Roscoe Conkling. In private life he is " the prince of good fellows" in the better sense of the phrase. No one more than he understand the beauty of the daily courtesies and little kindnesses which go so far toward pleasant living.

PRESIDENT GRANT'S FIRST CABINET.

Secretaries of State.—Elihu B. Washburne, of Illinois, appointed March 5th, 1869 ; Hamilton Fish, of New York, appointed March 11th, 1869.

Secretary of the Treasury.—George S. Boutwell, of Massachusetts, appointed March 11th, 1869.

Secretaries of War.—John A. Rawlins, of Illinois, appointed March 11th, 1869 ; William W. Belknap, of Iowa, appointed October 3d, 1869.

Secretaries of the Navy.—Adolph E. Borie, of Pennsylvania, appointed March 5th, 1869 ; George M. Robeson, of New Jersey, appointed June 25th, 1869.

Secretaries of the Interior.—Jacob D. Cox, of Ohio, appointed March 5th, 1869 ; Columbus Delano, of Ohio, appointed November 1st, 1870.

Postmaster-General.—John A. J. Creswell, of Maryland, appointed March 5th, 1869.

Attorneys-General.—Ebenezer R. Hoar, of Massachusetts, appointed March 5th, 1869 ; Amos T. Akerman, of Georgia, appointed June 23d, 1870; George H. Williams, of Oregon, appointed January 10th, 1872.

LEROY F. YOUMANS.

CHAPTER XXII.

CAMPAIGN OF 1872

REPUBLICAN NOMINEES.

For President.
ULYSSES S. GRANT of Illinois.

For Vice-President.
HENRY WILSON of Massachusetts.

LIBERAL REPUBLICAN DEMOCRATIC NOMINEES

For President.
HORACE GREELEY of New York.

For Vice-President.
B. GRATZ BROWN of Missouri.

CONVENTIONS AND NOMINATIONS.

THE Liberal Republicans, an organization which sprung from the Republican party in 1870, met in national convention at Cincinnati on the 1st of May, 1872, and nominated Horace Greeley and B. Gratz Brown.

The Democratic party, in its national convention held at Baltimore, July 9th, indorsed the nominations made by the Liberal Republicans at Cincinnati.

This action of the Baltimore Convention not being altogether acceptable to the more conservative element of the party, a convention was called at Louisville on the 3d of September by the Straight-Out Democrats, and

Charles O'Conor, of New York, and Charles Francis Adams, of Massachusetts, were placed in nomination.

The Labor Reform party held a convention at Columbus, Ohio, on the 21st of February, and nominated David Davis, of Illinois, for President and Joel Parker for Vice-President.

These nominees having declined, a convention of workingmen was held at Philadelphia on the 22d of August, and nominated Charles O'Conor, of New York, for President.

The Republican party held a national convention at Philadelphia on the 5th of June, and nominated General Ulysses S. Grant and Henry Wilson.

WADE HAMPTON.

General Wade Hampton was born in Columbia, South Carolina, on the 28th day of March, 1818. He is descended from Revolutionary stock, his great-grandfather having been an officer in the Revolutionary War. His family from that time to the present have occupied a prominent position in the history of South Carolina, both politically and socially, and up to the time of the late Civil War were possessed of large wealth.

The present General Wade Hampton lived upon his plantation near Columbia, and did not come prominently before the public until the Secession movement in 1861, when he cast his fortunes with those of his State, and enlisted in the cause of the Confederacy, and fought through the war until its close. His leadership and military qualities were early recognized, and he was rapidly promoted, and at the close of the Rebellion ranked as one of the most prominent generals on the Southern side.

After the war he returned to South Carolina and sought the quietude of his plantation, where he resided until called from his retirement by the unanimous voice of the people of the State to lead them in the exciting contest of 1876, when war upon what was known as "carpet-bag rule" was declared. He was nominated for governor at the Democratic Convention held at Columbia in the summer of that year against Daniel H. Chamberlain, the Republican nominee. The greatest enthusiasm prevailed after the nomination of Hampton, and the people took hope that a brighter future was opening for the State.

After the most spirited canvass ever held in the State Hampton carried the election, which was contested by the Republicans, but was finally decided by the inauguration of General Hampton as governor. The excitement and partisan feeling which prevailed during this contest was intense, Federal troops being stationed at Columbia at the time, which further embittered the people, and bloodshed was only prevented by the forbearance, wise counsel, and influence exerted by Wade Hampton under the most trying circumstances. The white people had the most unbounded confidence in his courage, wisdom, and ability, and he possessed in no small degree the confidence and respect of the colored population ; and, as events have proved, he was most worthy of the trust reposed. He was twice elected governor and since elected to the United States Senate, in which capacity he is now serving the State. In person Wade Hampton is an exceptionally handsome man, being over six feet in height, broad and well proportioned, and possessing a fine open and benevolent countenance.

He is an earnest speaker, carrying the conviction to every mind that he believes and means what he says. He ranks as one of the best political orators in his State, and it is only necessary to announce him on any occasion to draw a large audience. In the Senate on several occasions he has shown himself not unworthy to compete with the boldest combatants in that body.

BENJAMIN F. BUTLER.

Benjamin F. Butler was born at Deerfield, New Hampshire, on the 5th day of November, 1818.

In a recent speech he spoke of his early life as follows : " My father died at sea. I never knew him, for I was a babe in arms. His vessel was lost, and he left my mother to bring up her children, and a hard struggle it was. One of those children (referring to himself) was so delicate in health and small in body that it was thought he might not be able to labor with his hands. The other two aided the mother to send him to school, and afterward to Waterville College, in Maine, and there, for three hours a day, he labored with his hands in a mechanic's shop and helped to earn his education."

He graduated in 1838, and commenced the practice of law at Lowell, Massachusetts, in 1841. His disquisitive mind very early led him to take an active interest in politics, and in his early manhood he espoused the principles of the Democratic party. In 1853 he was elected a member of the Massachusetts House of Representatives, and six years later to the State Senate. In 1860 he was a delegate to the Democratic National Convention which met at Charleston, where he became conspicuous as a bold and fearless advocate of the principles which he maintained, and won a reputation for temerity which he has upheld with unfaltering consistency.

In the Charleston Convention, he endeavored to persuade the delegates to simply reaffirm the principles enunciated in 1856 at Cincinnati by the convention, which nominated Mr. Buchanan for the Presidency, but in this he was defeated. When a portion of the delegates reassembled at Baltimore, Mr. Butler, after taking part in the opening debates and votes, announced that a majority of the delegates from Massachusetts would not further participate in the deliberations of the convention, on the ground that there had been a withdrawal in part of the majority of the States ; and for himself, he added, " I would not sit in a convention where the African slave trade, which is piracy by the laws of my country, is approvingly advocated."

In the same year he was nominated by the Democratic party for the Governorship of Massachusetts, but was defeated by the Republican nominee, John A. Andrew.

When President Lincoln called for troops in April, 1861, General Butler held the commission of brigadier-general of militia. He was engaged in court at Boston when Governor Andrew received a requisition from the War Department for Massachusetts' quota of men, and in two days later General Butler marched out of Boston Common at the head of his brigade, leading his command to the defence of the Government. In the service of his country in the field, he distinguished himself no less than he had done by his ability in civic life. During the war General Butler underwent a change of political faith, and retired from the army a staunch Republican. In two or three campaigns after the close of the rebellion he was one of the most popular orators that addressed vast political meetings.

In 1866 General Butler was elected by the Republicans a member of Congress, and on taking his seat soon became a prominent and active member of the House of Representatives. He was the most active of the managers appointed in 1868 by the House of Representatives to conduct the impeachment of President Johnson. He closed his Congressional career in 1879.

In 1871, and every year successively until 1882, General Butler was an unsuccessful candidate for the Governorship of Massachusetts. In the latter year he was elected to that office by the Democrats, and defeated for a second term, in 1883, by the Republican nominee.

In 1884 he was a candidate for the Presidential nomination before the Democratic Convention at Chicago, having been previously nominated for that office by the National Greenback and Labor Reform parties. Failing in a nomination at Chicago, he subsequently wrote letters accepting the nominations tendered him by the Greenback and Labor parties, and thereupon became their regular nominee for the Presidential office.

General Butler has the courage of his convictions. He does as little as any public man for policy. If he wishes an office or political preferment, and it is not tendered him, he asks for it.

STEWART L. WOODFORD.

Stewart L. Woodford was born in the city of New York on the 3d of September, 1835. His father, Josiah C. Woodford, was from Hartford County, Connecticut; his mother from Suffolk County, New York. At the age of fifteen years he entered the freshman class of Columbia College, from which he graduated, third in his class, in 1854. He then devoted himself to the study of the law at New York City, and was admitted to the bar in 1857.

In the year 1860 he was delegate at Chicago to the convention which nominated Abraham Lincoln for the Presidency, and took an active part in the canvass which led to Mr. Lincoln's election. It was his privilege to convey the vote of the Electoral College of New York to Washington, and immediately after he was elected chairman of the Young Men's Republican Committee of the city of New York.

In 1861 Mr. Woodford was appointed Assistant United States Attorney for the Southern District of New York, and was placed in charge of the cases of naval captures, which were then very numerous, owing to the blockade of Southern ports. But in 1862, after McClellan's retreat from Richmond, he resigned this position to enlist as a private in the army. He was immediately elected captain of his company, which was assigned to the One Hundred and Twenty-seventh New York Volunteers, under Colonel

William Gurney. Before leaving for the front he was promoted to a lieutenant-colonelcy, and about this time he removed his residence to Brooklyn.

The winter of 1862-63 was spent by his regiment in and around Washington, which was then threatened by the rebel forces. On General Longstreet's investment of Suffolk, Virginia, in the spring of 1863, Colonel Woodford's command was sent thither and subsequently to the Peninsula under General Dix. He afterward served in the Eleventh Corps, and was then transferred to the Department of the South, where, with his regiment, he took part in General Gillmore's extensive operations against Charleston. He commanded, in the spring of 1864, the several forts on Morris Island which so destructively shelled Charleston. During the summer of that year he acted as Judge Advocate-General in the Department of the South, and in the early autumn of that year he was intrusted with the supervision of the exchange of prisoners in Charleston Harbor. But preferring active service, he applied for and received leave to rejoin his regiment and participate in the operations undertaken by General Foster against the Charleston and Savannah Railroad, and received commendation for his conduct at the battles of Honey Hill, Coosawhatchie, and Tulafinny.

Just before the surrender of Lee, and after active measures had ceased on the coast, Colonel Woodford was appointed Provost Marshal-General of the Southern Department, and was soon after made the first military Governor of Charleston, where he was successful in restoring and maintaining order and establishing an efficient local city government.

Major General Gillmore now appointed him his chief of staff, and while acting in this capacity he was brevetted brigadier-general for meritorious services. Shortly afterward he was appointed Military Governor of Savannah, which office he successfully filled, re-establishing the police force, relighting the streets, and satisfactorily administering generally the civil affairs of the city. He subsequently reassumed the position of chief of staff to the department commander, and in August, 1865, he resigned his commission, returning to his residence in Brooklyn and to the practice of the law in New York City.

In October, 1865, General Woodford was unanimously nominated by the Republicans of New York City as their candidate for Judge of the Court of Common Pleas, but he declined the nomination, not desiring to change his place of residence from Brooklyn.

In the fall of 1866, after a spirited canvass, in which he took an active part, visiting nearly every county in the State, he was elected lieutenant-governor by a majority of 15,024 votes over his Democratic competitor, Mr. Pruyn.

In 1870 he was nominated as Republican candidate for Governor of New York, but was defeated by the Democratic nominee, John T. Hoffman. In 1872 he was elected member of Congress from the Third Congressional District in Brooklyn, succeeding his old army comrade, General Henry W. Slocum. In the fall of that year he was chosen Presidential elector at large for New York, and on the assembling of the Electoral College, which cast the vote of the State for Grant and Wilson, he was unanimously elected by that body as its President. Frederick Douglass, also an elector at large, was chosen messenger to carry the vote to Washington.

In 1873 Mr. Woodford resigned his seat in Congress on account of professional business.

In 1875 he canvassed Ohio in joint debate on the money question with General Ewing, in the heated campaign of that year, which resulted in a victory for "honest money."

At the National Republican Convention in 1876 he received sixty-eight votes as a candidate for the nomination for Vice-President, but withdrew his name when the roll-call reached the State of New York.

In January, 1877, he was appointed United States Attorney for the Southern District of New York, and this being an office in the line of his profession, he accepted.

At the Republican National Convention of 1880 his name was again presented for the nomination for the Vice-Presidency, but he again withdrew, and nominated General Arthur.

In May, 1881, his term as district-attorney having expired, he was reappointed by President Garfield to that position, from which he was removed by President Arthur in the spring of 1883.

In addition to his active labors in his profession of the law, General Woodford has devoted much time to literary pursuits. He is still a careful student of the classics and an orator of recognized merit and ability.

PRESIDENT GRANT'S SECOND CABINET.

Secretary of State.—Hamilton Fish, of New York, continued.
Secretaries of the Treasury.—William A. Richardson, of Massachusetts, appointed March 17th, 1873; Benjamin H. Bristow, of Kentucky, appointed June 4th, 1874.
Secretaries of War.—William W. Belknap, of Iowa, continued; Alphonso Taft, of Ohio, appointed March 7th, 1876; James Donald Cameron, of Pennsylvania, appointed May 22d, 1876.
Secretary of the Navy.—George M. Robeson, of New Jersey, continued.
Secretaries of the Interior.—Columbus Delano, of Ohio, continued; Zachariah Chandler, of Michigan, appointed October 19th, 1875.
Postmasters-General.—John A. J. Creswell, of Maryland, continued; James W. Marshall, of Virginia, appointed July 3d, 1874; Marshall Jewell, of Connecticut, appointed September 1st, 1874; James N. Tyner, of Indiana, appointed July 12th, 1876.
Attorneys-General.—George H. Williams, of Oregon, continued; Edwards Pierrepont, of New York, appointed May 15th, 1875; Alphonso Taft, of Ohio, appointed May 22d, 1876.

WILLIAM MAHONE.

CHAPTER XXIII.

CAMPAIGN OF 1876.

REPUBLICAN NOMINEES.

For President.
RUTHERFORD B. HAYES of Ohio.

For Vice-President.
WILLIAM A. WHEELER of New York.

DEMOCRATIC NOMINEES.

For President.
SAMUEL J. TILDEN of New York.

For Vice-President.
THOMAS A. HENDRICKS of Indiana.

CONVENTIONS AND NOMINATIONS.

THE Republican National Convention was held at Cincinnati on the 14th of June, and nominated Rutherford B. Hayes and William A. Wheeler.

The National Convention of the Democratic party was convened at St. Louis on the 27th day of June, and nominated Samuel J. Tilden and Thomas A. Hendricks.

The "National" or "Greenback" party held a convention at Indianapolis on the 17th of May, and nominated Peter Cooper, of New York, for President and Samuel F. Cary, of Ohio, for Vice-President.

THOMAS A. HENDRICKS.

Thomas Andrews Hendricks was born near Zanesville, Muskingum County, Ohio, September 7th, 1819. His father was John Hendricks, a native of Western Pennsylvania, one of the first settlers of the Ligonier Valley, in Westmoreland County, and an active participant in public affairs, serving in the State Legislature and in other positions of trust. The mother was Jane Thomson, of Scotch descent, her grandfather, John Thomson, emigrating to America before the Revolution, and bearing an honorable and conspicuous part in that struggle. When Thomas was but six months old his father removed to Indiana, settling at Madison, on the Ohio River. This was the home of his brother, William Hendricks, the second governor of the new State, the first Representative in Congress, and afterward the predecessor of his more famous nephew in the United States Senate. John Hendricks held a minor office under the Government as surveyor of public lands, and was a man of good abilities and sturdy character. In the year 1822 the father of Thomas concluded to move further into the interior of the State, and took up his residence in Shelby County, near the present site of the county seat, Shelbyville. Here John Hendricks built him a substantial brick house, which is still standing, in which his family was reared, amid the best influences that could be enjoyed in those pioneer days. Indianapolis had just been laid out and established as the future capital of the State, and Mr. Hendricks's house was one of the principal centres of educated refinement in the central part of Indiana.

Thomas attended the village school until of sufficient age to enter the college at South Hanover, near Madison, graduating from which he began the study of law with Judge Major, the leading member of the bar of Central Indiana. The final period of his study was passed in the office of his uncle, Judge Thomson, of Chambersburg, Pennsylvania, and he was then admitted to the bar at Shelbyville. His success was not rapid; but his close attention to study, correct methods, and pleasant manners—all conduced to make him a favorite, and in the end he gained a high place in his profession and a lucrative practice. He was an impressive public speaker, having early given himself much to the arts of oratory, and this fact at once directed toward him the choice of the people for public life.

After five years' practice, in 1848, young Hendricks was elected to the Legislature, when not twenty-eight years of age. He was not particularly well pleased with that service, and declined a re-election in 1850. In the mean time a constitutional convention had been called, and though so young, the votes of the Senatorial district in which he lived elected him a member, he being one among the younger members of that body, with Schuyler Colfax and William S. Holman.

In August, 1851, he was elected to a seat in Congress from the central district of the State. His opponent was Colonel Rush, of Hancock, whom he defeated by nearly 4000 votes. By the terms of the new State Constitution an election was held the next year, in 1852, and again he was elected from a new district, his opponent being Mr. Bradley, an able and brilliant Whig, between whom and Mr. Hendricks in that campaign there was a joint discussion, the first of that sort of campaigning in Indiana.

On the 4th of March, 1855, Mr. Hendricks returned to his law office at Shelbyville, and in August of that year, while sitting on the porch of his home in the evening, a messenger stepped up and handed him an official autograph letter from President Pierce, making him the tender of the office of Commissioner of the General Land Office. Mr. Hendricks accepted the position, and in September appeared in Washington. He held this office until 1859, when he resigned and returned to the practice of his profession in Shelbyville.

But he was not allowed to remain quiet. His party was preparing for the great contest of 1860, and Mr. Hendricks was unanimously nominated by the Democratic Convention as candidate for governor, his opponent being the late Colonel Henry S. Lane, who had for his lieutenant Oliver P. Morton, who had four years previously made a brilliant but unsuccessful campaign against Ashbel P. Willard. The result was the election of Lane and Morton, and Mr. Hendricks returned to his law practice. He removed to Indianapolis shortly afterward and opened an office, taking at once a leading place at the bar.

The Legislature of 1862-63 was Democratic, and Jesse D. Bright having been expelled from his seat in the United States Senate, David S. Turpie was elected to fill out eighteen days of the unexpired term, while Mr. Hendricks was unanimously chosen for the full term of six years. He took his seat in the National Senate on the 4th of March, 1863, and served until 1869—four years as the colleague of Senator Lane and for two years with Senator Morton. He became in great measure the leader of the small

Democratic minority in that body. While yet a Senator in Congress his party again nominated him for governor, the Republicans nominating Conrad Baker. After an exciting campaign Baker was elected by about 800 majority, and Senator Hendricks again returned to his law office.

In 1872 the State was again rent with a political contest. The Liberal movement of that year on the part of dissatisfied Republicans gave the Democracy an apparent opportunity for success, and again the State Convention nominated Mr. Hendricks for governor. His Republican opponent was General Thomas M. Browne. As the result of another remarkably close election, Mr. Hendricks was chosen governor by a plurality of 1200 votes, while all the other officers of the State, except the Superintendent of Public Instruction, were Republicans. In the next month Grant carried Indiana by 6000 majority. He made an urbane, careful, satisfactory governor, and retired from the position with the respect of all parties in the State.

He was a candidate for the Presidency in 1868 at the New York Tammany Hall Convention, but there he was antagonized by a part of his own State delegation. He was again a Presidential candidate in 1876; but Samuel J. Tilden was the choice of the convention, and he accepted a nomination for second place.

Mr. Hendricks was again a candidate for the Presidential nomination at Cincinnati, in 1880, and this time had the ardent and enthusiastic support of his entire State delegation, but the nomination went to General Hancock. Mr. Hendricks worked ardently for the success of General Hancock, and his voice was heard in eloquent appeals in all sections of the country.

Mr. Hendricks was again a prominent candidate for the Presidency before the Chicago Convention in 1884; but the convention favored the claims presented by the friends of Grover Cleveland for that nomination, and Mr. Hendricks was thereupon nominated by a unanimous vote for the office of Vice-President.

CARL SCHURZ.

Carl Schurz was born at Liber, near Cologne, Prussia, on the 2d of March, 1829. He was educated at the Gymnasium of Cologne and the University of Bonn, which he entered in 1846.

At the outbreak of the revolution of 1848 he joined Gottfried Kinkel, professor of rhetoric in the university, in the publication of a liberal newspaper, of which for a time he was the sole conductor. In the spring of 1849, in consequence of an unsuccessful attempt to promote an insurrection at Bonn, he fled with Kinkel to the Palatinate, entered the revolutionary army as adjutant, and took part in the defence of Rastadt. On the surrender of that fortress he escaped to Switzerland. In 1850 he returned secretly to Germany, and with admirable skill and self-devotion effected the escape of Kinkel from the fortress of Spandau, where he had been condemned to twenty years' imprisonment. In the spring of 1851 he was in Paris, acting as correspondent for German journals, and he afterward spent a year in teaching in London. He came to the United States in 1852, resided three years in Philadelphia, and then settled in Madison, Wisconsin. In the Presidential canvass of 1856 he delivered speeches in German in behalf of the Republican party, and in the following year was defeated as a candidate for Lieutenant-Governor of Wisconsin. During the contest between Mr. Douglas and Mr. Lincoln for the office of United States Senator from Illinois, in 1858, he delivered his first speech in the English language, which was widely republished. Soon after he removed to Milwaukee and began the practice of law. In the winter of 1859-60 he made a lecture tour in New England, and aroused the attention by a speech delivered in Springfield, Massachusetts, against the ideas and policy of Mr. Douglas. Mr. Schurz was an influential member of the Republican National Convention of 1860, being largely instrumental in determining that portion of the platform relating to citizens of foreign origin, and spoke both in English and German during the canvass which followed.

President Lincoln appointed him minister to Spain, which post he resigned in December, 1861, in order to enter the army. In April, 1862, he was commissioned brigadier-general of volunteers, and on June 17th assumed command of a division in the corps of General Franz Siegel, with which he took part in the second battle of Bull Run. He was made major-general March 14th, 1863, and at the battle of Chancellorsville commanded a division of General Howard's corps, which was routed by General Jackson. He had temporary command of the Eleventh Corps at the battle of Gettysburg, and subsequently took part in the battle of Chattanooga.

On the close of the war he returned to the practice of law. In 1865-66 he was the Washington correspondent of the New York *Tribune*, and in

1866 he made a report, as special commissioner appointed by President Johnson, on the condition of the Southern States, which was submitted to Congress. In the same year he removed to Detroit, where he founded the Detroit *Post*; and in 1867 he became editor of the *Westliche Post*, a German newspaper published in St. Louis. He was temporary chairman of the Republican National Convention in Chicago in 1868, and labored earnestly in the succeeding canvass for the election of General Grant. In January, 1869, he was chosen United States Senator from Missouri, which office he held until the close of his term, in 1875. He opposed some of the leading measures of General Grant's administration, and in 1872 took a prominent part in the organization of the Liberal party, presiding over the convention in Cincinnati which nominated Horace Greeley for the Presidency. He was an active worker throughout that canvass. He visited Europe in 1873 and again in 1875, being received with marked consideration in his native country. On his return he took part in the political canvass in Ohio, in which he strenuously opposed the increase of the national currency. Mr. Schurz supported the Republican Presidential ticket in 1876, and was made Secretary of the Interior by President Hayes on the 12th of March, 1877. This office he held until the inauguration of General Garfield, in March, 1881, when he removed to the city of New York and entered upon the chief editorship of the *Evening Post*. Mr. Schurz was an eloquent advocate of the Republican ticket in 1880. In 1884 he became one of the leaders of a faction of the Republican party denominated Independents. Mr. Schurz's utterances are always listened to with great interest. A deep voice, with a rich German accent and perfect modulation, makes him a speaker of great eloquence.

Among his most celebrated speeches is an eulogy on Charles Sumner, delivered in Boston in 1874. Being asked by a lyceum bureau to repeat it at five hundred dollars a night, he replied he "did not speak on the memory of his friend for pay."

ALBERT MILLER CARD.

Albert Miller Card was born in the town of Ancram, Columbia County, New York, on July 21st, 1845, and is related to the Hon. Theodore Miller, of Columbia County, who is now a judge of the Court of Appeals.

He removed to Sharon, Connecticut, when quite young, and after attending the public schools of that town for some years, he graduated from the Sharon High School in 1861. He was then offered a position as teacher, which he accepted. Young Card's taste ran to the law, however, and he soon removed to Poughkeepsie, New York, where he entered the law office of the Hon. Charles Wheaton. In less than a year his progress was so great that he was admitted to the bar, and began the practice of law in Dutchess County. He had been a Democrat from his infancy, and soon began to take an active part in politics. His bright and sparkling oratory soon became famous in the neighboring counties, and he was always in demand at political gatherings. President Andrew Johnson appointed Mr. Card to the office of United States District Revenue Assessor, with headquarters at Poughkeepsie. He was also elected a school commissioner of Dutchess County on the Democratic ticket. Mr. Card then ran for Assembly against Warden Augustus A. Brush, now of Sing Sing Prison, but was defeated. Mr. Card removed to New York City in 1870, and associated himself with the Hon. Homer A. Nelson, then Secretary of State.

Mr. Card continued to take an active part in politics, and has established a wide reputation as an orator of great ability and magnetism. In the campaign of 1864 he was on the stump for three months in the interest of General George B. McClellan, and in 1876 he labored energetically for Tilden and Hendricks. His clarion voice was raised for Hancock and English in 1880, when he spoke all through the State and in several places in New Jersey.

The young man of to-day bewails the sad fate which has placed him in a degenerate age. The better qualities are not appreciated in this busy, money-making time : to succeed in politics one must have moral faculties of a low order ; that honesty in politics is an unknown quantity ; that ideas are nothing when pitted against the cunning of the ward politician or the moneyed monopolist.

This is fallacious. To-day, as ever, ideas rule. To-day a periodical edited with brains and conscience does more, in a single issue, to mould public opinion than the machinations of ignorant politicians through a protracted mud-throwing campaign. We do not decry the necessary party organizations. Demagogues find a large and profitable field in advocating " Civil Service Reform," much as it is needed. Organization is as necessary in politics as in the church ; and an attempt to do away with this is but a second Quixotic demolishment of a wind-mill.

A young man with ideas and courage can accomplish as much now as in any of those "good old times" so often sighed for, but which were worse than ours. To-day is better than yesterday. To-morrow will be better than to day.

Mr. Card, in conjunction with other thoughtful politicians, recognizes this, and cheerfully gives his time in an effort for the betterment of the political body, believing that pure politics insures liberty and honesty.

JOHN A. LOGAN.

John A. Logan was born on a farm in Jackson County, Illinois, on February 9th, 1826. Here he labored as a boy. His educational advantages were limited to the common school in his neighborhood ; but being possessed of a high order of natural ability, he read all the English works of sterling merit that he could buy or borrow, and in early manhood he had acquired a liberal fund of useful information. At the first call to arms in the Mexican War he enlisted as a private soldier in the First Illinois Volunteers. He was soon promoted to the post of quartermaster, with the rank of first lieutenant, and held the position during the war. Returning to Illinois he studied law with his uncle, A. M. Jenkins. After holding the position of clerk of the courts in his native county for a short time, General Logan entered the university at Louisville, graduating in law in 1852. He rapidly won his way to prominence in his profession. Political life attracted him, and in the fall of the same year he was elected to the State Legislature. From 1853 to 1857 he was prosecuting attorney, and in 1856 was Presidential elector in the Democratic party. From 1858 to 1861 he was a Representative in Congress, and in the midst of his unexpired term of office he enlisted and carried a musket in the first battle of Bull Run. Soon afterward he resigned his seat in the House, returned home, and raised a regiment for the war in September, 1861. As its colonel he led his soldiers to the front. At Belmont, Missouri, under Grant, though compelled to retire, Logan proved himself a leader of men. The battles of Fort Henry and Fort Donelson followed quickly, and General Logan, then advanced to the rank of major-general, was in the brunt of the fight with his regiment. He was wounded at Fort Donelson. He was at the battles of Pittsburg Landing and Shiloh, and took active part in the

James G. Blaine.

operations that followed. During the Vicksburg campaign he commanded a division of the Seventeenth Army Corps, taking a prominent part in the engagements at Port Gibson, Champion Hill, and the investment of Vicksburg. These were all hotly-contested battles. Personal bravery under fire and coolness and good judgment in danger characterized his actions, and made him popular with the soldiers. Under General W. T. Sherman he marched at the head of his division to the siege of Atlanta, and Sherman in his official report commended his bravery. The highest praise from General Sherman was elicited by the skilful manner in which General Logan, after the fall at Atalanta of the gallant General McPherson, in command of the Army of the Tennessee, assumed the position in the face of the enemy and in the confusion of battle. General Logan's biographers paint his picture on that day as riding up and down in front of the battle line, his black eyes flashing fire, his long black hair streaming in the wind, bareheaded, and his service-worn slouch hat swinging in his bridle hand and his sword flashing in the other, crying, in stentorian tones, "Boys, McPherson and revenge!" The fortunes of the day were with the Federal troops, but General Logan had been appointed in an emergency, and he retired from the command of the army, as General Howard had been appointed to the position.

After the fall of Atlanta General Logan returned to Illinois and took part in the Presidential campaign, speaking for Lincoln in halls, churches, and in the open air. When General Sherman, on his march to the sea, arrived at Savannah, General Logan rejoined his corps. In South Carolina his corps saved the State capital from destruction by fire. When in North Carolina, in the early part of 1865, General Logan succeeded General Howard in the command of the Army of the Tennessee, and he remained at the head of the army until the surrender of Lee, taking part in the grand review in Washington when the Union armies were disbanded. Then he returned to the practice of the law, and in 1866 he was elected Congressman at large from Illinois by a large majority, and re-elected in 1868, and in 1871 was chosen United States Senator. Failing in a re-election to the Senate in 1877, he resumed the practice of law in Chicago. In 1879 he was returned to the Senate, and now holds a seat in that dignified body. General Grant received his hearty support for a third presidential term, but as Garfield was nominated General Logan gave him his allegiance.

As an orator, General Logan is one of the most popular in the Western States. His striking personal appearance fixes attention to his utterances.

He does not care to employ the charms of rhetoric. The lighter graces of oratory are forgotten. To overwhelm his opponent is his object, and, convinced himself that he brushes away every opposing argument in his onward rush, he charges as if leading against an enemy's line of battle. His enunciation is clear and rapid, and his sentences gather force until they reach a climax at the close. In matter he is argumentative and convincing. His greatest speech in Congress was in opposition to the Fitz-John Porter bill. General Logan was nominated for the office of Vice-President at the National Republican Convention held at Chicago in June, 1884.

PRESIDENT HAYES'S CABINET.

Secretary of State.—William M. Evarts, of New York, appointed March 12th, 1877.

Secretary of the Treasury.—John Sherman, of Ohio, appointed March 8th, 1877.

Secretaries of War.—George W. McCrary, of Iowa, appointed March 12th, 1877 ; Alexander Ramsay, of Minnesota, appointed December 12th, 1879.

Secretaries of the Navy.—Richard W. Thompson, of Indiana, appointed March 12th, 1877 ; Nathan Goff, Jr., of West Virginia, appointed January 6th, 1881.

Secretary of the Interior.—Carl Schurz, of Missouri, appointed March 12th, 1877.

Postmasters-General.—David M. Key, of Tennessee, appointed March 12th, 1877 ; Horace Maynard, of Tennessee, appointed August 25th, 1880.

Attorney General.—Charles Devens, of Massachusetts, appointed March 12th, 1877.

CHAPTER XXIV.

CAMPAIGN OF 1880.

REPUBLICAN NOMINEES.

For President.
JAMES A. GARFIELD of Ohio.

For Vice-President.
CHESTER A. ARTHUR of New York.

DEMOCRATIC NOMINEES.

For President.
WINFIELD SCOTT HANCOCK of Pennsylvania.

For Vice-President.
WILLIAM H. ENGLISH of Indiana.

CONVENTIONS AND NOMINATIONS.

THE Republican party met in national convention at Chicago on the 2d of June, and nominated General James A. Garfield for President and General Chester A. Arthur for Vice-President. General Garfield was nominated on the thirty-sixth ballot. General U. S. Grant was a prominent candidate before this convention for a third Presidential term.

The Democratic National Convention was held at Cincinnati on the 22d of June, and General Winfield S. Hancock and William H. English received the nominations for President and Vice-President.

A national convention of the Greenback party met in the city of Chicago on the 9th of June, and chose as candidates for the offices of President and

Vice-President, respectively, James B. Weaver, of Iowa, and Benjamin J. Chambers, of Texas.

The Temperance or Prohibition party chose for its candidates, in a national convention held at Cleveland on the 17th of June, Neil Dow, of Maine, for President and A. H. Thompson, of Ohio, for Vice-President.

JAMES A. GARFIELD.

James Abram Garfield was born in Cuyahoga County, Ohio, on the 19th of November, 1831. His paternal ancestors came from England and settled at Watertown, Mass., in 1635. His father, Abram Garfield, was born in New York; his mother, Eliza Ballou, in New Hampshire. In 1830 they moved to Ohio and settled in the Orange woods, then a dense forest, broken only by occasional clearings of settlers. Here, in 1833, Abram Garfield died, leaving a family of four children, of whom James was the youngest, depending upon the exertions of a widowed mother. His boyhood was spent in laboring on the farm, to assist in the support of the family, and in attending the pioneer district school about three months each winter. When fourteen years of age he learned the carpenter's trade. His seventeenth summer was passed as a driver and helmsman on the Ohio Canal. His early ambition was to become a sailor, but a three months' attack of fever and ague, contracted on the canal, changed the current of his life into literary channels. In March, 1849, he entered Geauga Seminary at Chester, Ohio, and at the close of the fall term was competent to teach a district school. From 1851, three years of his life were passed in the Eclectic Institute at Hiram, performing at first the double duties of student and janitor, afterward of student and teacher. His earnings, which by the closest economy he had saved at Hiram, did not cover his expenses at Williams College, and he left college with a debt of five hundred dollars, which he afterward faithfully discharged. On his return to Ohio he accepted the professorship of ancient languages and literature in Hiram College. The next year, at the age of twenty-six, he was made its president, which office he held till he entered the army, in 1861. During this term he made frequent public addresses, both from the platform and pulpit, and established the reputation of being a felicitous speaker.

In 1859 he was elected to the Ohio Senate. His well-known characteristics as a legislator, his effectiveness as a debater, and his thoroughness as a committee man, were manifested in his career in that body. General Garfield's military services covered a period of two years and three months. He was mustered into service August 16th, 1861, and resigned his commission in the army on taking his seat in the Thirty-eighth Congress, December 5th, 1863, having been elected while absent in the field the year before a Representative from the Nineteenth Congressional District of Ohio. His ability and bravery as a soldier were recognized by the War Department in an order promoting him to the rank of major-general of volunteers "for gallant and meritorious services at the battle of Chickamauga."

He was re-elected to the Thirty-ninth Congress, and successively held that office until January, 1880, when he was chosen by the Ohio Legislature to succeed the Hon. Allen G. Thurman in the United States Senate. He served on the Committee of Military Affairs during his first term in the House of Representatives, and made one of his strongest and most effective speeches in favor of granting to Mr. Lincoln the power which he asked for drafting men to fill up the ranks, and it was largely due to the influence of this speech that a resolution to that effect was carried through the House. In the Thirty-ninth Congress he was assigned to the Committee of Ways and Means, and at once entered upon those financial studies which made him an authority on American finance. On the 15th of May, 1868, he made a speech on "The Currency," which is regarded a sound money manual and a cyclopædia of financial facts. After James G. Blaine's election to the United States Senate, in June, 1876, General Garfield became and continued to remain, till the end of his Congressional career, the acknowledged leader of the Republicans in the House. His speech in June, 1876, in reply to Mr. Hill, of Georgia, on the General Amnesty Bill, and his reply to Mr. Lamar, of Mississippi, August 4th, won for him the reputation of being the ablest and most forcible speaker in the halls of Congress.

On the 5th of June, 1880, General Garfield attended the National Republican Convention at Chicago as a delegate and as the champion of the Hon. John Sherman, whom he presented to the convention in a remarkably brilliant and effective speech, the opening portion of which is quoted, as follows : " Mr. President, I have witnessed the extraordinary scenes of this convention with deep solicitude. Nothing touches my heart more quickly than a tribute of honor to a great and noble character ; but as I sat in my seat and witnessed this demonstration, this assemblage seemed to me a human ocean in tempest. I have seen the sea lashed into fury and tossed into spray—and its grandeur moves the soul of the dullest man—but I remember that it is not the billows, but the calm level of the sea, from which all heights and depths are measured. When the storm has passed and the hour of calm settles on the ocean—when the sunlight bathes its peaceful surface, then the astronomer and surveyor take the level from which they measure all terrestrial heights and depths. Gentlemen of the convention, your present temper may not mark the healthful pulse of our people. When your enthusiasm has passed—when the emotions of this hour have subsided, we shall find below the storm and passion that calm level of public opinion, from which the thoughts of a mighty people are to be measured, and by which their final action will be determined.

"Not here, in this brilliant circle, where fifteen thousand men and women are gathered, is the destiny of the Republic to be decreed for the next four years ; not here, where I see the enthusiastic faces of seven hundred and fifty-six delegates, waiting to cast their lots into the urn and determine the choice of the Republic, but by four millions of Republican firesides, where the thoughtful voters, with wives and children about them, with the calm thoughts inspired by love of home and country, with the history of the past, the hopes of the future, and reverence for the great men who have adorned and blessed our nation in days gone by burning in their hearts—*there* God prepares the verdict which will determine the wisdom of our work to-night. Not in Chicago, in the heat of June, but at the ballot boxes of the Republic, in the quiet of November, after the silence of deliberate judgment, will this question be settled. And now, gentlemen of the convention, what do we want ? [A voice. 'We want Garfield.'] Bear with me a moment. 'Hear me for my cause,' and for a moment ' be silent that you may hear.'"

The convention heard him through to the end of his grand peroration, and later, notwithstanding his protests that he was not a candidate, made him its Presidential nominee. He was elected " in the quiet of November, *after the silence of deliberate judgment,*" and inaugurated President of the United States on the 4th of March, 1881. He had scarcely embarked on his administration before he was stricken down by an assassin's hand. From the fatal wound which he received on the 3d of July, 1881, he was a brave and heroic sufferer until the 19th of September following, when he passed away. The life of Garfield is the fullest exemplification of the possibilities of American citizenship. He began life in the Ohio forest, poor in earthly store, and by his own exertions, abilities, and character, he made his way upward to the highest place. His path led him by the log-house district school, carpenter's shop, tow-path, academy, and college to the Legislature, the army, the House of Representatives, the United States Senate, and to the chief magistracy of the nation.

LEROY F. YOUMANS.

Leroy Franklin Youmans was born on the 14th day of November, 1834, in that part of the District of Beaufort now known as Hampton County, in the State of South Carolina.

He received his academical education in the Beaufort District Academy; from this institution he entered the sophomore class of the South Carolina College in December, 1849, and graduated with distinction in December, 1852.

He was admitted to the bar in January, 1856, and practised at the Beaufort Court until the breaking out of the war between the States in co-partnership with Mr. Edmund Rhett, a brother of Robert Barnwell Rhett, a United States Senator from South Carolina. Immediately upon his admission to the bar Mr. Youmans took a high position, and was, almost at his first term, complimented by Mr. Petigru, who predicted for him a distinguished career, the promise of which he has thus far eminently fulfilled. The first Presidential campaign in which he was engaged was that of 1860; but the State being unanimous for Breckenridge, there was no necessity for any special exertion on his behalf.

Mr. Youmans served in the Confederate Army throughout the war, from its beginning to its close, although, as a member of the House of Representatives of the General Assembly of the State, he was exempt from service.

He was appointed solicitor in the year 1866 by Governor Orr, and was afterward elected to that office without opposition by the Legislature. Mr. Youmans made the last speech in defence of the parish system of South Carolina, in the convention called by Governor Perry in 1865.

In September, 1867, he moved to Edgefield, South Carolina, where he practised law for five years in partnership with General M. C. Butler, now

United States Senator, until Butler's removal to Columbia, and for some time afterward as partner of John C. Sheppard, since Speaker of the House of Representatives, and now Lieutenant-Governor of South Carolina. He took part on the Democratic side for Seymour and Blair in the Presidential campaign of 1868, and spoke in different parts of the State.

In the South Carolina State Reform campaign of 1870 he spoke throughout the State for the reform candidates, R. B. Carpenter for governor and M. C. Butler for lieutenant-governor, against R. K. Scott and A. J. Ransier, the Republican candidates, who were successful.

In the fall of 1872 he removed to Columbia, where he has ever since practised law as the partner of William K. Bachman.

He took no part in the Presidential campaign of Grant, Greeley, and O'Conor in 1872.

In the Presidential campaign of 1876 he spoke throughout the State, and took a most active part for the Democratic candidates, Tilden and Hendricks, against Hayes and Wheeler, the Republican nominees; and for Wade Hampton, now United States Senator, and William D. Simpson, since governor and now Chief-Justice of South Carolina, Democratic candidates for governor and lieutenant-governor, against D. H. Chamberlain, then governor, and R. H. Gleaves, then lieutenant-governor, Republican candidates—the most exciting political contest ever waged in the State.

He was of counsel for the Tilden electors and for the Democratic candidates for the State officers in the long-protracted and most exciting semi-political litigation ever brought before the Supreme Court of the State. The masterly document entitled "Reply of Wade Hampton, Governor of South Carolina, and others, to the Chamberlain Memorial" was from the pen of Mr. Youmans.

He was of counsel for the prisoners in the cases growing out of what are so widely known as the Ellenton Riots, tried in the spring term of 1877 before Chief-Justice Waite, of the Supreme Court of the United States, and Bond, Circuit Judge at Charleston, South Carolina.

His efforts on this occasion commanded the admiration of all who heard him, and were spoken of in terms of unqualified eulogy in the papers of the State, as follows: "The admirable effort of Leroy F. Youmans, Esq., in defence of the Ellenton prisoners, at the trial in Charleston, is regarded as the finest specimen of eloquence, reasoning, sarcasm, and illustration heard in the legal forum for many days.

His earnest and fervid defence of the people of South Carolina against

Chauncey M. Depew.

the mad aspersions of unscrupulous enemies, from within and without, and his scathing denunciation of the means employed to secure the conviction of innocent men, will entitle him to the unending gratitude of every citizen of the State."

In December, 1877, Mr. Youmans was unanimously chosen by the General Assembly of the State attorney-general to fill the vacancy caused by the resignation of General Conner, and was the nominee of the Democratic party, without opposition, for that office in 1878 and again in 1880, and was on both occasions elected by the vote of the people of the State. The resignation of the office of attorney-general by General Conner elicited the following complimentary tribute to Mr. Youmans by the *News and Courier*, the leading paper of the State : " The successor of General Conner will be elected by the General Assembly. Mr. L. F. Youmans, who fought by the side of General Conner in the forensic battles last winter, and was his worthy associate in the late trials in Columbia, is the most prominent candidate." And his appointment by the General Assembly gave rise to the following highly appreciative remark of the same paper : " Leroy F. Youmans, the new attorney-general, is an erudite lawyer and as eloquent and cogent a pleader as can be found at the Southern bar. During the canvass last year he labored with conspicuous zeal and ability for the success of the Democratic cause, but his great services in the political arena are dwarfed into insignificance by his masterly work in court during the proceedings for the enforcement of the title of the Democratic candidates, and by the research, power, and sagacity he exhibited in the preparation and argument of the cases against Smalls, Cordoza, and Carpenter."

His career as attorney-general of the State was 'one continued series of brilliant and masterly forensic efforts, conspicuous among which was his arguments, in Boston, on the requisition for Kimpton. Of that, among other very complimentary notices, the *Nation* of that day said : " Mr. Youmans's forensic oratory is of a kind that has not been heard in Massachusetts for many years, not so much because it is Southern, as because it marks a period as remote from us as Webster and Benton."

He spoke in different parts of the State in the State campaign of 1878, and in the Presidential campaign of 1880 for Hancock, and in the State campaigns of 1880 and 1882. He declined a re-election to the office of attorney-general, and has since that time devoted himself to his private practice. In the election trials at Columbia, 1883, he was said to have surpassed any of his former great efforts. He was a delegate from the State at large to the Democratic Convention at Chicago in July, 1884, where he seconded the nomination of Mr. Bayard in a brilliant and eloquent speech, which was a marked feature of the convention.

JOHN SHERMAN.

John Sherman was born in Lancaster, Ohio, on May 10th, 1823. His father, Judge Charles R. Sherman, of the Supreme Court, died, leaving Mrs. Sherman with eleven children and no income. Mr. Sherman's cousin, also named John Sherman, a grocer in Mount Vernon, took the boy to his home, and kept him in school until he was twelve years old. John was a leader in mischief and in sport, but he managed somehow to avoid castigation by the teacher. Then he returned home, and after studying for two years in the academy in Lancaster, accepted the position of junior rodman on an engineer corps engaged in improving the Muskingum River. While on this work, in the enforced idleness of the winter of 1838–39, he entered into a disastrous speculation in salt, which was for a long time a subject of joke among his kindred and friends. The future financier, whose name stands next to that of Alexander Hamilton in that respect, failed flat in his first venture in handling money. He purchased a lot of salt, and had it loaded on a scow, intending to float down to Cincinnati with it and sell it at a profit. Unfortunately, when the scow was within one day's journey of the mouth of the river, it was frozen in the ice, and remained there for two months. When spring arrived the price of salt had dropped in Cincinnati, and Sherman lost money. In 1839 he was thrown out of his position for political reasons. Then he wanted to enter college, but could get no money. His brother, Charles Sherman, who practised law in Mansfield, Ohio, invited his stalwart young brother, then nineteen years old, to study law in his office.

Mr. Sherman was admitted to the bar on May 17th, 1844, at Springfield, Ohio, and at once became a partner with his brother, Charles T. Sherman. From that time until 1854, when he was elected a member of Congress, he was constantly, actively, and profitably employed in the practice of his profession. His style of oratory before a jury was not of the florid, ornamental type, but a plain, blunt, straightforward presentation of facts. Instead of indulging in the full, round, oratorical tone, his voice was sunk to a conversational key. The effect on his hearers was as though his thoughts were spontaneous, and he was quietly drawing all the law and the facts of the case from his client.

The venerable plain brick residence in which Mr. Sherman now lives in Mansfield was built in 1849. On the corner porch, as seen from the front, Mr. Sherman rests in summer evenings. The house is set in well-kept grounds and surrounded by a variety of shade-trees.

In the winter of 1854 Mr. Sherman established a law office in Cleveland. It was at the time of the agitation—North and South—over the Missouri Compromise, and Mr. Sherman, who had been a conservative Whig, was nominated by a joint convention of Democrats, Whigs, and Free-Soilers as Representative in Congress, and he was elected. Before he took his seat he assisted in the formation of the Republican party in Ohio. He soon commanded the respect of his associates and the confidence of his political friends. When he arose to debate he showed a full comprehension of the subject, the result of careful and dispassionate examination, and his familiar acquaintance with public affairs gave weight to his words. His strong common-sense, a result of the balance of his faculties, made him equal to every emergency. His stoutest political foes found cause to respect his weighty reasoning, while his best friends found him unalterably attached to his convictions.

The turning-point in Mr. Sherman's career was his appointment, by Speaker Nathaniel P. Banks, on a committee to visit Kansas, in 1856, and collect evidence in regard to the election frauds practised by advocates of slavery. A state of violence amounting to civil war existed. The committee took their testimony in the presence of men armed and ready to fight. Notices, with drawings of skull and cross-bones at the top, threatening violence to the committee, were found posted on the doors of the committee-room. The committee's report, compiled by Mr. Sherman, was the basis of the Republican campaign of 1856. On the side of the minority Mr. Sherman began his career in advocating economy in public expenditures. His attitude was that of watchdog of the national treasure-house, not by obstructing necessary appropriations, but by a careful, thorough, and logical course of reasoning. At the close of his second Congressional term he was recognized as the foremost man in the House of Representatives.

At the breaking out of the war he was first to advocate raising funds at a high rate of interest, if necessary, to sustain the national credit and carry on the conflict. His speeches in favor of the Union were an appeal to reason. He believed that disunion meant a military despotism and perpetual conflicts between the North and the South.

President Lincoln's first meeting with Mr. Sherman was in Washington, at the time Lincoln went to Washington previous to his inauguration. "And so you are John Sherman," was Lincoln's first salutation after shaking hands. He stepped back and measured Mr. Sherman with his eye. "Well," he said, "I am taller than you are, anyway." They backed up against each other, and Lincoln was declared to be two inches the taller. From that time their acquaintance was of a friendly nature.

Mr. Sherman had just been elected to a seat in the Senate, and from the time Fort Sumter was fired upon until July, when Congress met in extra session, Mr. Sherman acted as General Patterson's aide-de-camp with the Ohio regiments. His great services to the Union cause were in his careful watch of the public finances and a support of the armies in the field. The caution of the financier was, however, in great critical moments swept aside in a patriotic speech. When foreign interference was hinted at, in 1862, he said: "Rather than yield—rather than bequeath to the next generation a broken Union, I would light the torch of fanaticism and destroy all that the labor of two generations has accumulated."

Mr. Sherman was the author and promoter of most of the great financial schemes of Government, from the beginning of the war to the present time. His greatest triumph was in paving the way to the successful resumption of specie payments, on January 1st, 1879. He had been Secretary of the Treasury under President Hayes for two years, and when he entered the Cabinet no step toward specie resumption had been taken by the Government. Apparently he alone had faith that it could be accomplished. A prominent financier in New York said he would give $50,000 to be at the head of the line at the Treasury building on the day specie payments were begun; but when the day arrived he could have had the whole street for nothing. To accomplish this result Mr. Sherman had to provide for the redemption in coin of nearly $350,000,000 in greenbacks. He was also successful in refunding the public debt at a low rate of interest. Since his retirement from the Cabinet Mr. Sherman has been successively elected to the Senate, and in times of popular political excitement he has taken the stump, and contributed facts, figures, and logic to the campaign. His enemies say he is an icy man. His friends maintain that he is a safe man to manipulate public affairs.

WILLIAM MAHONE.

General William Mahone was born in Southampton County, Virginia, December 18th, 1826. He graduated with distinction at the Virginia Military Institute in July, 1847, and taught school the two ensuing years. Relinquishing the vocation of a teacher, he was appointed civil engineer on the Fredericksburg Plank-Road and the Orange and Alexandria Railroad, and in 1852 was appointed chief engineer of the Norfolk and Petersburg Railroad, and was elected president of the company in 1856. He was colonel of the Sixth Virginia Volunteers, Confederate service, brigadier and major-general successively of the brigade and division which bore his name, serving with distinction from the capture of the Norfolk Navy-Yard, in 1861, to the surrender of Lee, in 1865.

General Mahone was elected State Senator during the war, but only occupied his seat a few days. He was a candidate for governor in 1877, and was elected United States Senator in 1881, since which time he has commanded a large share of public attention. From 1865 to 1869 Virginia had no status in the Union other than "Military District, No. 1." In the latter year she was restored to fellowship in the sisterhood of States, when a Bourbon and a Radical Republican, each a typical representative of his party, were candidates for the governorship, and the election of either foreboded harmful results to Virginia in her condition at that time. The Bourbons hated the Federal Government, and the Radicals hated the whole people of the South. At this juncture William Mahone, till then a lifelong Democrat, appeared prominently on the political stage, and with the assistance of sober-minded Republicans, Whigs, and Democrats united in the nomination of a Liberal candidate, who was elected. It was from this coalition that the Conservative party of Virginia sprang, and which General Mahone was instrumental in forming.

In 1877 General Mahone was induced to become a candidate for governor, and entered the convention of fourteen hundred delegates with sixty less than a majority over all his rivals ; but quickly perceiving the doubtful chance of his own nomination on the first ballot, and realizing the necessity of scoring a quick and decisive victory over all his competitors, he wrote a ticket, gave the signal, and his candidate was nominated on the first ballot, and was subsequently elected governor. In 1879 General Mahone entered the canvass for the Legislature, opposed by the whole machinery of the Conservative party, which was in the hands of the Bourbons—the governor whom he had named two years before, all the corporations, and the Federal office-holders—but he carried the State by a very large popular majority of over 20,000, and he was subsequently elected to the United States Senate as a Readjuster.

His tireless efforts to heal the wounds which the war had inflicted, and bring prosperity to his State, was a sufficient earnest to the people of Virginia that he had their welfare at heart. He entered the Senate untrammelled with pledges, and said to the Administration supporters : " The people, in the exercise of their sovereign will, have placed the executive control of their affairs at the national capital in the hands of a Republican President. I am here to promote the popular judgment—to aid the Administration as it may please to allow. It should have the opportunity of prosecuting its own policy by a friendly organization of the Senate, on this basis, as you may deem appropriate. I demand and expect nothing." In this he is supported by his constituents. Educated in a school of science and trained in a purely scientific profession, he attempts none of the arts and accomplishments of rhetoric and oratory. His style of speech is plain, terse, and vigorous, and of that character which commands attention. In person General Mahone is delicately framed, but he possesses a wonderful capacity for work and endurance. His weight is about 115 pounds. Strong in his own convictions, he parleys with no "slow of foot" nor wastes time with grumblers or bolters. He uses his political power in the interest of no personal friendship ; his heart is in the promotion of the public good and the preservation of the integrity of his party.

PRESIDENT GARFIELD'S CABINET.

Secretary of State.—James G. Blaine, of Maine, appointed March 5th, 1881.

Secretary of the Treasury.—William H. Windom, of Minnesota, appointed March 5th, 1881.

Secretary of War.—Robert T. Lincoln, of Illinois, appointed March 5th, 1881.

Secretary of the Navy.—W. H. Hunt, of Louisiana, appointed March 5th, 1881.

Secretary of the Interior.—S. J. Kirkwood, of Iowa, appointed March 5th, 1881.

Postmaster-General.—Thomas L. James, of New York, appointed March 5th, 1881.

Attorney-General.—Wayne McVeagh, of Pennsylvania, appointed March 5th, 1881.

PRESIDENT ARTHUR'S CABINET.

Secretary of State.—Frederick T. Frelinghuysen, of New Jersey, appointed December 12th, 1881.

Secretary of the Treasury.—Charles J. Folger, of New York, appointed October 12th, 1881.

Secretary of War.—Robert T. Lincoln, of Illinois, continued.

Secretary of the Navy.—William E. Chandler, of New Hampshire, appointed April 12th, 1882.

Secretary of the Interior.—Henry M. Teller, of Colorado.

Postmasters-General.—Timothy O. Howe, of Wisconsin, appointed December 20th, 1881; Walter Q. Gresham, of Indiana, appointed April 6th, 1882.

Attorney-General.—Benjamin Harris Brewster, of Pennsylvania, appointed December 16th, 1881.

CHAPTER XXV.

CAMPAIGN OF 1884.

REPUBLICAN NOMINEES.

For President.
JAMES G. BLAINE of Maine.

For Vice-President.
JOHN A. LOGAN of Illinois.

DEMOCRATIC NOMINEES.

For President.
GROVER CLEVELAND of New York.

For Vice-President.
THOMAS A. HENDRICKS of Indiana.

CONVENTIONS AND NOMINATIONS.

The Republican party, in national convention held at Chicago on the 5th of June, nominated for the office of President James G. Blaine and for the office of Vice-President General John A. Logan. Mr. Blaine was nominated on the fourth ballot; General Logan by acclamation.

The Democratic National Convention was held in the same city on the 8th of July, and selected as candidates for the two highest executive offices Grover Cleveland and Thomas A. Hendricks. Mr. Cleveland was nominated on the second ballot; Mr. Hendricks by acclamation.

ROBERT G. INGERSOLL.

JAMES G. BLAINE.

James Gillespie Blaine, the candidate of the Republican party for President in the contest of 1884, is a descendant of a race of hardy Scotch Presbyterians, who settled in Western Pennsylvania about the time of the close of the Revolutionary War, there contesting with the Indians the right of possession, and wresting from the soil enough to sustain life. His grandfather was an officer in that struggle, winning deserved honors, and his father was an able and just local magistrate. James G. Blaine was born on the 31st of January, 1830, at West Brownsville, Washington County, in that State, and remained there, attending school regularly, until his father removed to the county seat, to fill the duties of an office to which he had been elected. At eleven years of age the son was sent to the house of a relative at Lancaster, Ohio, that relative being Thomas Ewing, then the Secretary of the Treasury, and a very well-known and powerful politician. Here he pursued his preparatory studies for college in conjunction with his cousin, Thomas Ewing, Jr., and in two years was able to enter Washington College, in Pennsylvania, from which, four years subsequently, he graduated with distinction. He was an active member of the literary society, spoke frequently upon all the questions which came before it, and was noted for having a fine memory. His kindly and generous nature was then confidently relied upon by his fellow-students when they needed assistance, and he was equally a leader in manly sports. Shortly after he was graduated he became a teacher in a military school in Kentucky, and during his residence there he became acquainted with and married his present wife, Miss Harriet Stanwood, and shortly thereafter returned to Pennsylvania. In 1852 he accepted the position of a teacher in the Pennsylvania Institute for the Blind, in Philadelphia, where he showed himself an apt instructor and a man of industry and statistical research. The school still preserves the record of its early history, which he compiled for it.

These ventures completed Mr. Blaine's preparatory course. He was now to be an actor in a larger field, and from being a preceptor of children he was to become a leader of men. Acting in obedience to the solicitations of his wife, who was from Maine, he removed to that State in the winter of 1854, buying a share in the *Journal*, a well-known Whig paper of

Kennebec. He was then only twenty-three years old, but he speedily acquired a great influence, not only in his own county, but also throughout the whole State. When he went there it was as the old Whig party was just dissolving, and his relations brought him into contact with all the leaders of the Republican party, anxious only for their country's good. At twenty-nine years of age he was the chairman of the executive committee of his organization for the whole State, a position which has been practically his ever since. He begun as a speaker about this time, and his election to Congress, which came when he was in his thirty-first year, made that gift of great value. Mr. Blaine as an orator is not of that stereotyped class of which General Cass, of Michigan, might have been taken as the example, using a diffuse, pompous, and ornate diction, even while having good sense, but he is rather of the school of Cobbett. Everything has a bearing and a meaning. His matchless memory enables him to choose his weapons with ease, and his skill in composition and in arranging facts places them in the best light. His orations are the quintessence of common sense. They are not elaborately built up and ornamented, but are of the same language that he uses at the fireside and in talking with his neighbors in country districts. In Congress his services grew very valuable. He had tact and judgment, and he supported his party thoroughly. He was elected again and again, and in 1870 was chosen Speaker of the House. His quickness, his extraordinary knowledge of parliamentary law, his historical researches, his fairness—all combined to make him one of the most remarkable men who ever occupied the seat once graced by a Clay and a Muhlenberg. Business was transacted with great quickness under his rulings, as he soon reached the heart of a subject, and was impatient at digressions on side issues. This important position he filled for six years, or until the party opposed to him gained the majority in the Lower House of Congress, a length of time surpassed by only two of his predecessors, and equalled by but two others. His address on leaving the chair was an able and affecting one, every word being fitly chosen. During the next session Mr. Blaine was the acknowledged leader of the Republicans in the House of Representatives. In June, 1876, Lot M. Merrill resigned his place as Senator from Maine to become Secretary of the Treasury, and Mr. Blaine was selected to fill the unexpired term, being re-chosen in 1881. He resigned his seat in the Senate on accepting President Garfield's invitation to a seat in his Cabinet. Thus was accomplished nineteen years of arduous service, in which he spoke on most important subjects, and acted on all. He defeated the attempt of Governor Garcelon and his followers to override the will of the voters of Maine ; he upheld the national faith in the currency ; but he especially distinguished himself in his advocacy of a tariff and protection to American labor. No public man of the day has spoken more frequently or fervently in advocacy of the principles of his party. Facts and figures are made plain and clear by him. He has opposed the admission of Chinese into this country as laborers, holding that as they now are they are unfit to become American residents or citizens. On all these subjects and on many others he has spoken freely, both in Congress and elsewhere, the addresses being models of composition and statement.

Mr. Blaine has three times been a candidate before his own party for the Presidency. In 1876 he competed with Morton, Conkling, Bristow, and Hayes, the last being the victor. In 1880 he was a strong rival to General Grant, General Garfield being finally nominated. This year he led the field, Senator Edmunds and President Arthur being his strongest rivals, and was finally nominated unanimously on the fourth ballot. He supported Mr. Hayes in his campaign, as well as General Garfield, four years after. Of the latter he was one of the warmest friends, and on Garfield's election he was selected as Secretary of State, filling the duties of that office with judgment and full regard for the rights of Americans abroad. When the shot was fired by the assassin, Blaine was by Garfield's side, and virtually directed the Government until his death. On President Arthur's accession he resigned, giving way to Mr. Frelinghuysen, and has since then been in retirement. He has not, however, been idle. His pen has been busy with a history of the Government and people of the United States from the accession of Lincoln to the death of Garfield, in which he has been singularly successful. The history is couched in a philosophic spirit, is clear and accurate, indulges in no reflections against those who have been on the opposite side to him, and is easy and pleasant reading. It is the general voice that he has surpassed his great predecessor, Senator Benton, in the skill and ability with which the work has been done. Mr. Blaine is now only fifty-three years old, and much may be expected of him in the future. As an orator, in which aspect we chiefly view him, he has been one of the most able and successful in the United States. Without having the magical power of Clay or Prentiss, he has the ability of clear and convincing statement, of cumulative illustration, of sarcasm, and of argument drawn from homely life that would make him a dangerous antagonist on any subject. But as he never speaks on a topic concerning which he is not fully informed, he is generally able to enforce his views on even the most unfavorable audiences. His style is not the ornate or the discursive; it bears directly upon the point at issue, and does not waste its force by blows in the air. Of American speakers on political or social subjects, he may justly claim to be regarded as among the first.

CHAUNCEY M. DEPEW.

Few among the younger men of America have achieved such prominence in oratory as Chauncey M. Depew, and if his ability may be tested by his powers to command the attention of a New York audience, there are scarcely none. Mr. Depew has not yet passed his half century, having been born in Peekskill, Westchester County, New York, of good old Huguenot stock, in the year 1837. His ancestors emigrated to this country after the revocation of the Edict of Nantes, at the same time the ancestors of the Jays, the Disosways, the Desbrosses, and the Delanceys came hither. He received the advantage of excellent training in school, and was sent to Yale College in 1852, completing his course and graduating in 1856. Among those who were his contemporaries at college were Andrew D. White, President of Cornell University, Warner, the humorist, and many other distinguished men. His abilities were recognized from a very early date, and he had important positions assigned to him at the meetings of college societies, at reunions, and on commencement day. He elected the study of the law, pursuing his studies under favorable auspices, and in 1859 began business for himself in New York City. Here his acuteness of perception and his flow of humor made him a universal favorite, and he soon began reaping a comfortable income. In 1863 the Republicans, in casting about for a man of parts and good character to head their State ticket, selected Mr. Depew as their candidate for Secretary of State, and he was triumphantly elected in November, taking his seat on the first of January following. The office of Secretary of State is not the most important one in the gift of the State, nor is it one of which the duties are very arduous, but it is considered the most dignified and desirable next to the office of governor. The most important function which he had to perform was in taking the census of 1865. Much apprehension then existed among the minds of laborers and workingmen as to the object of this inquisition, and many endeavored to evade answering the questions. But the rules laid down by Mr. Depew proved to work admirably in practice, and the results were copious and accurate, far surpassing those of the United States census of five years before. After retiring from this office, at the close of 1865, he again began the practice of the law, but soon received an offer from the New York Central Railroad Company to act as their counsel in cases where litigation was feared, and accepted their proposition, acting in this capacity ever since. Two years ago, when the New York Central was reorganized by the withdrawal of Mr. William H. Vanderbilt from daily duties as president, Mr. Depew was chosen second vice-president. In 1877, in consideration of his position as a college man and a lover of education, he was chosen a Regent of the University. He became noted for his skill as a speaker early in life, and each year that has passed has seen his talents improve. He possesses an unequalled faculty of placing a subject in a humorous form, and frequently is able by this ability to shed new light upon a question which had previously seemed to have but one side. His political speeches are models of oratory. The whole vocabulary of the language seems to be under his command, and the words marshal themselves into line with the utmost ease; he uses apt illustrations, is never disconcerted by interruptions, and carries on the even tenor of his argument, mixed with grave or gay allusions, with scarcely an effort. Perhaps no public man of the day speaks in public with less labor. You cannot conceive of him as beginning a sentence that he cannot finish, or of making an argument which will not have its weight. During the past dozen years Mr. Depew has spoken before college societies, the Chamber of Commerce, boards of arbitration, and the press of America, and on countless topics. Each one is handled with fulness and grace. His latest set speech was before the Produce Exchange, when it opened its magnificent new temple of commerce, the grandest now existing on the globe, in which he bitterly denounced the speculators and those who traded in a way to inflict injury upon the community. No other orator, probably, could have held that audience so long and so thoroughly. In after-dinner speeches every sentence, almost, is greeted with a roar of laughter, and his invitations to attend social gatherings are so numerous that he is compelled to decline nearly all of them. Mr. Depew is a man of thorough and solid parts; as a lawyer he ranks among the leaders of the New York bar, and his skill as a railroad man is of vast use to the stockholders of the New York Central. He has often been mentioned for the highest offices in the gift of the State, and three years ago was the choice of a large number of Republicans for their representative in the United States Senate. He is still younger than most of those who have already occupied this position, and his friends believe that the time will soon come when the seat once occupied by Silas Wright and William H. Seward shall worthily be filled by him.

ROBERT G. INGERSOLL.

At a great political meeting held at the Academy of Music, in the city of Brooklyn, on the night of the 30th of October, 1880, the Rev. Henry Ward Beecher concluded an introductory of Colonel Ingersoll to the vast audience as follows : " The gentleman who is to speak to you to-night is not speaking in a conventicle nor in a church. He is speaking in a great body of citizens, and I take the liberty, in your behalf, to say now that we greet him to-night as a man who has done valiant things for the right, without variableness or shadow of turning, for a full score of years. On the ground of a pure patriotism, of a pure humanity, and of a living faith in liberty, I give to him the right hand of fellowship. (*At this juncture Mr. Beecher gave Mr. Ingersoll his hand.*) Now, fellow-citizens, let me introduce to you a man who, I say not flatteringly, but with sincere conviction, is the most brilliant speaker of the English tongue in any land on the globe."

Colonel Ingersoll was born at Dresden, a picturesque village on the west bank of Seneca Lake, in the State of New York, on the 11th of August, 1833. After completing a classical education, he studied law, and located at Peoria, Illinois. His magnetic nature very speedily drew clients and a lucrative practice, and thus, under most auspicious circumstances, he commenced the voyage of life.

His captivating speech, nominating James G. Blaine in the Cincinnati Convention in 1876, first brought him into national prominence. That effort he concluded as follows : " Gentlemen of the convention, in the name of the great Republic—the only Republic that ever existed upon this earth—in the name of all her defenders and of all her supporters—in the name of all her soldiers living—in the name of all her soldiers dead upon the field of battle—and in the name of those who perished in the skeleton clutch of famine at Andersonville and Libby, whose sufferings he so vividly remembers, Illinois—Illinois nominates for the next President of this country that prince of parliamentarians, that leader of leaders, James G. Blaine." Before the campaign of that year had closed, every one in the land was familiar with the name and fame of the genial and brilliant orator, Colonel Robert G. Ingersoll.

The subjects which he discusses in political addresses are systematically arranged, and so admirably presented with striking features, that a vivid picture of the situation is impressed upon the minds of his auditors.

At a great meeting which he addressed in Cooper Union, New York, he gave his views on what he believed should be the standard of money as follows:

" I am in favor of honest money. I am in favor of gold and silver, and paper with gold and silver behind it. I believe in silver, because it is one of the greatest of American products, and I am in favor of anything that will add to the value of an American product. But I want a silver dollar worth a gold dollar, even if you make it or have to make it four feet in diameter. No government can afford to be a clipper of coin. A great republic cannot afford to stamp a lie upon silver or gold. Honest money, an honest people, an honest nation. When our money is only worth eighty cents on the dollar, we feel twenty per cent below par. When our money is good we feel good. When our money is at par that is where we are. I am a profound believer in the doctrine that for nations, as well as men, honesty is the best, always, everywhere and forever. What section of this country, what party, will give us honest money—honor bright—honor bright? I have been told that during the war we had plenty of money. I never saw it. I lived years without seeing a dollar. I saw promises for dollars, but not dollars. And the greenback, unless you have the gold behind it, is no more a dollar than a bill of fare is a dinner. You cannot make a paper dollar without taking a dollar's worth of paper. We must have paper that represents money. I want it issued by the Government, and I want behind every one of these dollars either a gold or a silver dollar, so that every greenback under the flag can lift up its hand and swear, ' I know my redeemer liveth.' "

In the winter of 1876-77 Colonel Ingersoll appeared upon the lecture platform, his subjects, under various titles, being attacks upon religion and denominational creeds. These lectures brought out replies from the pulpit and religious press all over the land ; but the country finally settled down to the conviction that Colonel Ingersoll's good nature so neutralized the shafts of ridicule which he aimed at Christianity, that the institution would suffer no serious harm from his attacks.

The Rev. Dr. Robert Collyer, a celebrated divine, relates a story that once a friend of Colonel Ingersoll called on him at his home in Peoria, and noticing a handsomely bound volume of Paine, took it from its library shelf, and asked the colonel what it cost him. The reply was, " It cost me the Governorship of Illinois." There can be little doubt that in that significant answer the distinguished orator mentioned one item and gave a key to many which his creed had cost him.

As a word painter, Colonel Ingersoll is an artist without a peer, and he has spoken sentiments than which no more beautiful or patriotic have ever been uttered. Closing a great speech, from which we have already quoted, he said : "Oh, I love the old Republic, bound by the seas, walled by the wide air, domed by heaven's blue, and lit with the eternal stars ! I love the Republic ; I love it because I love liberty. *Liberty is my religion,* and at its altar I worship and will worship."

THE END.